COOKING WITH NATURAL FOODS II

as you search for abundant health

Muriel Beltz
BLACK HILLS HEALTH & EDUCATION CENTER
Box 19, Hermosa, South Dakota 57744

MMI
Books

Aldworth Road ● P.O. Box 279
Harrisville, NH 03450

Library of Congress Card Number: 89-061877
ISBN 0-912145-18-8

Printed by
MMI Press
P.O. Box 807
Harrisville, NH 03450

1st Edition – December 1989

Additional copies may be obtained from Muriel Beltz.
Order coupons are in the back of this book.

Contents

Health is a Treasure

"Happy is the person that findeth wisdom and getteth understanding, for that is the way of pleasantness and peace." See Proverbs 3:13, 17.

"Blessed art thou, O land, when . . . thy princes eat for strength and not for drunkenness." Ecclesiastes 10:17

Many do not realize the importance of temperance and regularity in all things which will promote sweetness and serenity of disposition.

Obedience to the laws of health is not a matter of sacrifice or self-denial but is a blessing.

Disease never comes without a cause. Disease is invited as the laws of health are disregarded. Many times it is because of the wrong habits of the parents that people suffer, but with a greater number it is because of their own wrong course of action. The principles of wellness are nature's laws of eating, drinking, dressing, and working. If one disregards natural law, suffering usually follows.

Each person is given a certain amount of vital force. If we carefully preserve the life force by keeping the delicate mechanism of the body in order, the result will be wellness.

When sickness comes because of the abuse of health the first thing to be done is to remove the cause. Overworking, overeating, or other irregularities may be causing the difficulties. Many times a fast of a meal or two will be the best remedy. This will give the overworked organs of digestion an opportunity to rest.

There are many ways that water can be applied to relieve pain and check disease—(See *Health and Fitness* compiled by Dr. M. E. Beltz).

Many times physical exercise would prove an effective remedial agent. To be of the greatest advantage it should be agreeable and systematic. Outdoor exercise is best. Enjoy it!

There is a so-called science based on false principles where one mind is brought under the control of another. One person acts out the will of another. The one who attracts minds to himself leads the other person to separate from the true Source of strength.

No one is to merge his individuality in that of another. No one is to look to any human being as the source of healing. His dependence must be in God. When the mind is turned away from God, it can be brought under the control of another power. What opportunity it affords to those who wish to take advantage of others' weaknesses! He who made man's mind knows what the mind needs, and God alone can heal. Cooperate with Him, obey the laws of wellness. He will give you power and strength.

The power of the will should be greatly valued. If kept awake and rightly directed it will impart energy to the whole being and it will be an aid in maintenance of wellness. Exercised in the right way it would be a means of resisting and overcoming disease of mind and body. Some invalids can rise above the aches and pains and engage in useful activities suited to their abilities. In this way, along with fresh air and sunlight, many persons might recover health and strength. When the sunlight of God's love illuminates the mind, restless weariness and dissatisfaction will cease and satisfying joys will give vigor to the mind and health and energy to the body.

Nothing tends more to promote health of body and mind than does a spirit of gratitude and praise. Look to the natural world and take time to gather some beautiful living flowers. Look at the beauty of the mountains—the valley clothed in living green—listen to the sweet and musical sounds of the wild creatures. Rejoice in the blessings received from appreciating the goodness and love of God.

Find ways to be helpful to others. Good deeds are twice a blessing, benefitting both the giver and the receiver of the kindness.

Many will never know the influence of their kind, considerate course toward the inconsistent and the unreasonable as they shed light on the dark pathway of those unacquainted with the better way.

Cultivate the habit of speaking well of others. Dwell upon the good qualities of those with whom you associate.

Do something every day to improve, beautify and ennoble the life that Christ has given you.

Without a knowledge of health principles, no one is fitted for life's responsibilities. Pure air, sunlight, abstemiousness, rest, exercise, proper diet, the use of water, trust in Divine Power—these are the true principles.

Life is a wonderful gift and health is a treasure.

PREVENTIVE CARE

PREVENTIVE CARE is a heart full of love
extended through us from God up above.
It is a freedom, a willingness to tell
of the things we know to keep you well.
We want you to know of our longing to share
God's remedies that are not rare—
but ABUNDANT and SWEET.

PREVENTIVE CARE is a new way of living
Our body responds and keeps on giving
days free of pain and sweet sleep at night,
which make the world more beautifully bright.
Use God's gifts and you will be
a better specimen of humanity.
BE GRATEFUL FOR THIS!

PREVENTIVE CARE will brighten your days and
add joy to your life in many ways.
With it you add a new dimension
life is simple, serene and without tension.
Judicious care has benefits plus,
for God made the rules and God made us.
A MIRACLE INDEED!

PREVENTIVE CARE—God had it in mind
from the very beginning to the end of time.
Eight natural remedies, so simple 'tis true,
and He made them all to care for you.
And now we say "Give God the Glory," and
share with others this wonderful story.
PRAISE HIS HOLY NAME!

Muriel Beltz

BLACK HILLS
HEALTH & EDUCATION CENTER

The Black Hills Health & Education Center Wellness Program is a program designed to give people an alternative in the prevention and treatment of disease. Located in the Black Hills of South Dakota, the Center is nestled in a valley surrounded with red-rim rock cliffs. A gentle stream flows through the center of the property. The fresh air, sunshine, and scenic beauty of the area make it an ideal place for people to rest, exercise, and learn the proper methods of disease prevention.

In the great majority of cases, disease is brought on by unhealthful lifestyle habits. Generally these habits are formed by following the accepted practices of our society, without understanding their hurtful consequences. We are paying billions a year for health care, forever seeking out doctors to patch up what many of us have done to ourselves by improper diet, smoking, lack of exercise, excessive use of alcohol, and stressful living.

Conventional treatment includes medicine to combat the disease or surgery to repair or remove diseased organs. While this is often a reasonable approach, the patient's long-range, total health is not assured if there is no accompanying change in the offending lifestyle. We need to take care of ourselves and learn how to shoulder more responsibility for our well-being in an intelligent way.

The health education program at Black Hills Health & Education Center is very simple: *CHANGE LIFESTYLE PATTERNS.* Replace debilitating habits with those that are more healthful, natural, and therapeutic . Emphasis is placed on health education or lifestyle medicine, an approach that will allow the guest to become a well-informed participant in his or her own recovery. The main theme in this program is to help people develop a lifestyle that will bring the entire body, physically, spiritually, and mentally into optimum health.

Previous experience indicates that persons may be helped—in varying degrees—who come under these general disease categories: cardiovascular (atherosclerosis, hypertension, claudication); inflammatory (arthritis); pulmonary (bronchitis); metabolic (obesity, diabetics, hypoglycemia, allergies); and others. This program is also indicated for post-cardiac surgery rehabilitation. People who have discovered through screening diagnostic procedures, that they are likely candidates for heart attack, stroke, diabetes, or similar preventable diseases, may find this program helpful. However, there is another group of people who can benefit more than any other group—those who choose to invest in preserving rather than recovering their health. Our educational thrust is ideal for those who wish to enhance and retain their good health.

This new lifestyle (new habits) is based upon intelligent application of nature's eight most available healing agencies. You will find a brief synopsis on each of these at the end of this book.

If you need further information about any phase of the **Black Hills Health & Education Center**, or would like to become a guest at a future **Wellness Program,** call 605-255-4579 or 605-255-4101. Write to: *Black Hills Health & Education Center, Box 19, Hermosa, South Dakota 57744.*

No Refined Fat or Refined Sugar
No Cholesterol
High in Bulk and Fiber,
Natural Protein
Vitamins and Minerals

COOKING WITH NATURAL FOODS II

as you search for abundant health

Murial Beltz, Black Hills Health & Education Center, Box 19, Hermosa, SD 57744

Dear Friends,

Thank you, dear friends! I want to take this opportunity to thank you, each of you, who have encouraged me in the compiling of the cookbook, **Cooking With Natural Foods** and now a new cookbook, **Cooking With Natural Foods II**.

You have expressed your appreciation and have sent recipes to be used in the cookbooks. Some have asked to have their recipe changed to make it more healthfully delicious and I hope this has been accomplished. I praise God for this.

Cooking With Natural Foods II is an entirely new book—different recipes and different suggestions and ideas. The basic recipes for a maintenance diet are in the first cookbook as well as much valuable information on a changed life style. The recipes in **Cooking With Natural Foods II** are in addition giving more variety to meal planning.

The first cookbook, **Cooking With Natural Foods**, featured the percentages of protein, fat and complex carbohydrates in most of the recipes and charts of Food Composition of Whole Foods (pages 18-22). By comparing recipes in the first book, one can estimate the value of protein, fat and complex carbohydrates. **Cooking With Natural Foods II** features quantity figures for 6-8 servings and 24-25 servings.

Therapeutic Recipes are marked with a (T). These recipes have approximately 10% protein, 10% fat and the balance complex carbohydrates. Grains, vegetables and fruits in their natural state are all therapeutic with these exceptions: avocados and olives. When nuts, including coconut, are added to the diet, the percentage of fat will increase to 20% or more—depending upon the amount of nuts. A good rule to follow is: Use only ⅙ - ¹⁄₁₀ part nuts in any product, or do not use more than one product per meal that is high in natural fat. Remember: Calories *in* must equal calories *expended* if proper weight is to be maintained.

Cooking With Natural Foods recipes are now available on cards in an attractive acrylic recipe box which has an acrylic shield to hold and protect the recipe when in use. We have had many requests for this, and those who have the **NATURAL FOODS RECIPE CARD COLLECTION** are excited about it. They still use their cookbook for reference for some of the information not on the cards.

Cards are also available for **Cooking With Natural Foods II** and these will fit into the acrylic box with the other cards.

We are delighted and thankful that we can offer these items to you and we trust that they will be of help to you as they make Cooking With Natural Foods more enjoyable and worthwhile each day.

Yours for healthful choices,

Muriel Beltz

Muriel Beltz

P.S. Remember when ordering—you must designate which cookbook you want and which set or sets of cards from the Recipe Card Collection.

FROM THE HOLY SCRIPTURES

This is the day, this is the day that the Lord hath made, that the Lord hath made;
We will rejoice, we will rejoice and be glad in it, and be glad in it.
This is the day that the Lord hath made; We will rejoice and be glad in it.
This is the day, this is the day that the Lord hath made.

Psalm 118:24

I beseech you therefore brethren, by the mercies of God, That you present your bodies a living sacrifice, Holy, acceptable unto God, Which is your reasonable service.

Romans 12:1

Know ye not that ye are the temple of God, and that the Spirit of God dwelleth in you: If any man defile the temple of God him shall God destroy; for the temple of God is holy, which temple ye are.

1 Corinthians 3:16, 17

What? know ye not that your body is the temple of the Holy Ghost which is in you, which ye have of God, and ye are not your own? For ye are bought with a price; therefore glorify God in your body, and in your spirit, which are God's.

1 Corinthians 6:19, 20

Beloved, I wish above all things that thou mayest prosper in health, even as thy soul prospereth.

III John 2

If thou wilt diligently hearken to the voice of the Lord thy God, and wilt do that which is right in his sight, and wilt give ear to his commandments, and keep all his statues, I will put none of these diseases upon thee, which I have brought upon the Egyptians: for I am the Lord that healeth thee.

Exodus 15:26

Who forgiveth all thine iniquities; who healeth all thy diseases.

Psalm 103:3

Whether therefore ye eat, or drink, or whatsoever ye do, do all to the glory of God.

I Corinthians 10:31

Behold, I have given you every herb bearing seed which is upon the face of all the earth, and every tree, in the which is the fruit of the tree yielding seed, to you it shall be for meat.

Genesis 1:29

WHY A DIET LOW IN FAT AND CHOLESTEROL CAN HELP YOU

Heart and blood vessel problems, such as angina and hypertension, disorders such as diabetes and hypoglycemia which involve the body's ability to handle sugar, and other ailments as well, are beginning to be recognized as being primarily due to the diet we consume. The diet eaten in advanced countries, such as the U.S., has a total fat content of 40-50% of calories consumed. It is also very high in refined carbohydrates. Scientific investigators have found in poorer countries, where the people eat a diet usually under 20% of total calories in fats consisting mainly of unrefined carbohydrates such as whole grains, fruits and vegetables, that these diseases are almost never found. In countries less poor, but not quite so advanced as ours, where the diet is in between, there is an in-between amount of these diseases. The more the fat and refined carbohydrates eaten, the more degenerative disease problems are found.

Other scientists have studied the effects of our typical diet in laboratories and clinics, and have confirmed the suspicion that the large amount of fat and refined carbohydrates consumed in this country can bring on these degenerative diseases; whereas a diet in which fat and refined carbohydrates are sharply curtailed can cause these disease symptoms to lessen and even to disappear completely.

The kind of fat does not seem to matter—the fats may be those from dairy products, such as in whole milk, butter, cheese, etc.; or in the form of vegetable fats as found in the oil of nuts, seeds, avocados, olives, and vegetable oil spreads such as margarine or nut butters; or fat as found in animal foods. It is the total amount of fat of all kinds that is consumed that matters; the more fat, the more disease symptoms.

In addition to the fat contained in them, animal muscle tissue of all kinds—beef, pork, lamb, poultry, fish, shellfish, etc., but especially organ tissue (liver, brains, kidneys, etc.) and eggs (chicken eggs, fish roe, etc.)—introduce still another harmful substance into our bodies: cholesterol. While some cholesterol is needed by the body, the body produces all that it requires. If additional cholesterol is added to the diet it becomes stored in the blood and tissues, since the body is unable to excrete it. In the presence of blood which has a high concentration of fat, the excess stored cholesterol in time causes lesions, called plaques, to form inside the blood vessels. This condition is known as atherosclerosis.

On our typically high fat diet, these plaques begin to form even in very young people, gradually building up over a period of time and narrowing the channels in the blood vessels. This narrowing of the blood vessels reduces the amount of blood flow to the tissues served by these vessels and, in time, the heart compensates by elevating the blood pressure more and more, producing high blood pressure or hypertension.

If the blood vessels that serve the heart (coronary vessels) become sufficiently clogged by plaques, any circumstance which further reduces the already diminished oxygen supply to the heart muscle will cause the heart to "cry out" in pain—the terrible pain of angina. A slight exertion such as running a short distance, an emotional episode, or even a single fat meal, can bring on an angina attack. In one experiment, the subjects, angina patients, did nothing but drink a glass of cream. Even though they were at complete rest, all of them suffered angina attacks.

A fatty meal reduces the oxygen supply to all of the body tissues, not only to the vessels serving the heart. This will happen even if your arteries are not clogged by plaques—though few adults are so lucky, unless they have been on a lifelong low fat, low cholesterol diet. Even in a baby, fat steals oxygen from the body cells. It steals oxygen from the tissues just as the carbon monoxide does when taken in by smoking. In the case of fat, this happens because of several mechanisms. When the digested fat is broken down, it forms tiny fat balls which tend to clump together in the bloodstream. These aggregate with solid elements in the blood and block the blood flow in the tiniest arteries, thus depriving the cells in the tissues, fed by those arteries, of needed oxygen nourishment. The tiny fat balls also coat these solid elements in the blood. As a result, the red blood cells that are the body's oxygen carriers become stuck together in formations resembling rows of coins. The clumping of the red blood cells further slows the circulation, depriving the tissues of even more oxygen. When the clumped red blood cells reach the lungs where they should take up oxygen from the air breathed in, being clumped together, much of their surface area is not free to pick up oxygen. In this way, much less oxygen is carried back into the tissues which are still further deprived of oxygen.

It is because of this process of depriving the body cells of oxygen that fats enable cholesterol to form the atherosclerotic plaques. The artery walls become more easily penetrated by fats and cholesterol when the blood that bathes them is deficient in oxygen, thus encouraging the plaques to form. On a high fat diet, the process of plaque formation goes on hour after hour, day after day, in all of the arterial vessels throughout the body. In the course of many years, the constant narrowing of these vessel channels by the evergrowing plaque formations causes many symptoms. High blood pressure and angina are two of the common symptoms; others include a gradual deterioration in hearing and vision and even senility and impotency.

In many studies, it has been shown that by going on a diet in which fat and cholesterol intake are sharply reduced, the plaque-forming process can be reversed and the symptoms produced by the artery damage lessened or even eliminated. Refined carbohydrates and added salt have been found to contribute significantly to the development of heart and blood vessel problems. On a low fat diet, the plaques or sores that are narrowing your arteries should gradually begin to disappear so that nearly normal circulation will be restored.

This same diet has proved successful in reversing diabetes and hypoglycemia. Hypoglycemia is a pre-diabetic stage, caused by similar abnormal conditions in the blood to those that bring about diabetes; both respond to the same dietary therapy—a low fat diet. Diabetes and hypoglycemia appear under the circumstances which occur when the concentration of fats in the blood is very high. By lowering the blood fats by a diet low in fats of all kinds, and low in simple carbohydrates, like sugar, honey and molasses, which become converted, a Canadian investigator, Dr. I. M. Rabinowitch, treated 1,000 diabetics over a five-year period and had a high rate of success. Even insulin-dependent diabetics no longer required insulin or other drugs in 25% of the cases. Had the diet been even lower in fat content, Dr. Rabinowitch would have obtained an even higher reversal rate, based on the experiences of others.

High blood fats bring about a situation where the insulin from the pancreas is unable to effectively act upon blood sugar. Studies have been done where perfectly normal young men were made diabetic in a period of days or even hours, depending upon how fast fats were introduced into their blood. When fats were introduced very rapidly, by injection into the bloodstream instead of by diet, they became diabetic in two hours. The scientists who did this study were also able to reverse diabetes by chemically lowering the blood fats.

You would lower your blood fats by a gradual and permanent means, by your diet; and the fast results you could obtain would surprise you if you adhered to the diet closely.

Certain kinds of arthritis also respond well to a diet by which blood fats are reduced. High blood fat levels cause the watery part of the blood (plasma) to seep out of the tiniest arteries (capillaries) at an abnormally high rate, due to the pressure built up in the capillaries when the circulation becomes slowed. The resultant swelling or edema produced in the tissues provides the environment conducive to the development of arthritic symptoms. When the edema and slowed circulation in the capillaries are improved, marked relief and recovery can occur. Other diseases also have shown an improvement on this type of diet, such as colitis, gallbladder disease, hypertension (high blood pressure), and obesity.

Your health, to a great extent, is dependent upon your lifestyle. Major risk factors are controllable. You must be in charge!

We suggest a diet without cholesterol, fat 10-20% of the calories, approximately 10% of the calories in protein, and about 70% of the calories from unrefined carbohydrates. Salt should be one-half teaspoon or less per day.

Good Sources of Fiber

Food	Serving Size	Grams of Fiber
Baked beans	½ cup	8.3
Broccoli, cooked	1 medium stalk	7.4
Coconut	2" x 2" x ½" piece	6.1
Spinach, cooked	½ cup	5.7
Blackberries	½ cup	5.3
Almonds	¼ cup	5.1
Apple	1 medium	4.5
Kidney beans	½ cup	4.5
Peas, cooked	½ cup	4.2
White beans	½ cup	4.2
Banana	1 medium	4.0
Corn	½ cup	3.9
Potato	1 medium	3.9
Pear	1 medium	3.8
Lentils	½ cup	3.7
Lima beans, cooked	½ cup	3.5
Sweet Potato	1 medium	3.5
Pinto beans	½ cup	3.1
Shredded wheat	1 biscuit	3.1
Peanuts, chopped	¼ cup	2.9
Brown rice, raw	½ cup	2.8
Corn flakes	1 cup	2.8
Orange	1 medium	2.6
Raisins	¼ cup	2.5
Brussels sprouts	4	2.5
Peanut butter	2 tablespoons	2.4
Apricots	3 medium	2.3
Carrot, raw	1 medium	2.3
Puffed wheat	1 cup	2.2
Beets	½ cup	2.1
Peach	1 medium	2.1
Cabbage, boiled, shredded	½ cup	2.0
Zucchini, raw	½ cup	2.0
String beans, raw	½ cup	2.0
Tomato, raw	1 medium	1.8
Barley, raw	½ cup	1.8
Whole wheat bread	1 slice	1.8
Plums	3 medium	1.8
Onions, cooked	½ cup	1.6
Strawberries	½ cup	1.6
Walnuts, chopped	¼ cup	1.6
Asparagus, chopped	½ cup	1.2
Cauliflower, raw	½ cup	1.0
Pineapple	3 ½" x ¾" piece	1.0
Asparagus	4 medium spears	.9
White bread	1 slice	.8
Cherries	10	.8
Celery, raw	1 stalk	.7
Onions, raw, chopped	¼ cup	.6

Good Sources of Calcium

Food	Serving Size	Milligrams
Lamb's quarters, cooked	½ cup	193
Collard greens, cooked	½ cup	193
Tofu, mashed	2 ½ cups	146
Brazil nuts	¼ cup	139
Spinach, cooked	½ cup	116
Kale, cooked	½ cup	103
Almonds, raw	¼ cup	82
Garbanzos (chick peas), cooked	¼ cup	75
Dandelion greens	½ cup	74
Soybeans, mature, cooked	½ cup	73
Beet greens, cooked	½ cup	72
Broccoli	½ cup	68
Sesame seeds	¼ cup	63
Lentils, cooked	½ cup	52
Figs	2 large	52
Blackberries	1 cup	46
Apricots, dried, cooked	1 cup	46
Red grapefruit	1	46
Beans, cooked	½ cup	45
Cherries, sweet, raw	1 cup	44
Parsley	½ cup	43
Papaya	½ large	40
Cabbage, cooked	½ cup	38
Pumpkin & squash seeds	¼ cup	29
Lima beans, cooked	½ cup	28
Cabbage, raw	½ cup	26
Boysenberries	1 cup	25
Brussels sprouts	½ cup	25
Raisins, dried	¼ cup	25
Green snap beans	½ cup	25
Pineapple, raw	1 cup	24
Celery	½ cup	23
Blueberries	1 cup	21
Peanut butter, natural	2 tablespoons	18
Green peas	½ cup	15
Pear, fresh	1 medium	15
Cashew nuts	¼ cup	13
Prunes	¼ cup	13
Banana	1 medium	12
Apple	1 medium	9

Good Sources of Iron

Food	Serving Size	Milligrams
Pumpkin & squash seeds	¼ cup	6.5
Apricots, dried, uncooked	½ cup	4.2
Garbanzos (chick peas), dry, raw	¼ cup	3.4
Lima beans	½ cup	3.0
Sunflower seeds	¼ cup	2.9
Brewer's yeast, dry	⅛ cup	2.8
Soybeans, mature, cooked	½ cup	2.7
Brazil nuts	¼ cup	2.5
Great Northern beans, cooked	½ cup	2.4
Soybeans, cooked	½ cup	2.4
Grape Nuts® (cereal)	½ cup	2.4
Kidney beans	½ cup	2.3
Cashews	¼ cup	2.0
Red kidney beans, cooked	¼ cup	2.3
Lentils, cooked	½ cup	2.1
Pears, dried	½ cup	1.9
Black-eyed peas	½ cup	1.8
Parsley, chopped, raw	½ cup	1.8
Jerusalem artichokes, raw	¼ cup	1.5
Almonds	¼ cup	1.4
Blueberries, raw	1 cup	1.4
Raisins, dried	¼ cup	1.4
Sesame seeds	¼ cup	1.4
Blackberries, raw	1 cup	1.4
Figs	2 large	1.3
Grapefruit 5" red	1 medium	1.1
Banana	1 medium	1.1
Spinach, steamed	½ cup	1.1
Boysenberries	1 cup	.9
Peas, frozen, heated	½ cup	.9
Collards, cooked	½ cup	.8
Cherries, sweet, raw	1 cup	.8
Pineapple	1 cup	.7
Pear, fresh	1 medium	.6
Broccoli	½ cup	.6
Apple, raw	1 medium	.4
Peanut butter, natural	2 T.	.3
Cabbage, shredded, cooked	½ cup	.3
Cabbage, shredded, raw	½ cup	.2

RDA   Male: 10 mg.
Female: 18 mg.

Good Sources of Zinc

Food	Serving Size	Milligrams
Pumpkin seeds	¼ cup	2.8
Peanuts	¼ cup	2.4
Cashews	¼ cup	1.9
Peanut butter	¼ cup	1.9
Sunflower seeds	¼ cup	1.8
Brazil nuts	¼ cup	1.6
Grape Nuts® (cereal)	½ cup	1.2
Black-eye cowpeas, cooked	½ cup	1.2
Lentils, cooked	½ cup	1.0
Soybean kernels, roasted	¼ cup	.98
Almonds	¼ cup	.96
Red kidney beans, cooked	½ cup	.9
Great Northern beans, cooked	½ cup	.9
Roman Meal, cooked	½ cup	.9
Walnuts	¼ cup	.7
Green peas, cooked	½ cup	.7
Wheat Chex® (cereal)	½ cup	.6
Rolled wheat cereal, cooked	½ cup	.5
Oatmeal (rolled oats, cooked)	½ cup	.5
Coconut	¼ cup	.4

MENUS

These suggested menus are guidelines for you to use in selecting foods for your family. *DO NOT* try to follow them exactly—you may find it necessary to substitute often. Use foods in season.

Set aside one day a week for baking bread, waffles, granola, rolls, crackers, pita, etc. Make two or three products a week and freeze the surplus for future use.

Set aside one day for making salad dressings, mayonnaise, nut butters, cashew jack cheese, spreads.

If you want a dessert, use one of your choice from the NATURAL SWEETS section, or some fresh fruit.

Foods never improve by canning or freezing, so use fruits and vegetables fresh as much as you can. For example, in strawberry season, use strawberries in fresh fruit pie, fruit salad, on your cereal, or just as they come from the market or garden.

Use a variety of foods. **Learn** to like food that is good for you. **Try** different vegetables and fruits. **Be thankful** for good, natural foods.

BREAKFAST	DINNER	SUPPER
Sunday		
Grapefruit	Potato Nests with	Zucchini Soup
Tomato Toast	Creamed Asparagus	Toast and Crackers
Whole Grain Toast	Beet & Walnut Salad	Rhubarb Strawberry Cobbler
Sesame Butter	Carrot Salad	Fresh Fruit
Fruit Jam	Cornmeal-Wheat Rolls	
Fresh Fruits	Kidney Beans & Garbanzo	
	Spread	
	Lemon Pie	
Monday		
Cooked Wheat Berries	Ideal Potatoes	Fresh Pea Soup
Almond Fruit Milk	Garbanzo Tomato Loaf	Whole Grain Toast & Crackers
Whole Grain Toast	Herbed Green Beans (or plain)	Fruit Spreads
Fruit Spreads	Salad Toss	Fresh Fruit
Fresh Fruits	Rye Biscuits & Cheese	
	Coconut Cookies	
Tuesday		
Sliced Oranges	Spaghetti Squash	Winter Squash Soup
Granola	Vegetable Sauce for Spaghetti	Toast & Crackers
Whole Grain Toast	Salad Bar or Toss Salad	Fresh Fruit Pie
Almond Butter	Whole Grain Bread	Fresh Fruit
Fruit Jam	Garbanzo Sesame Spread	
Fresh Fruit	Tofu Delight	
Wednesday		
Rolled Oat & Rye, Rolled	Noodle Casserole	Millet Soup
Wheat	Three-Bean Salad	Whole Grain Toast & Crackers
Granola	with Cumin Dressing	Fruit Spreads
Almond Milk	Bread - Herb with	Fresh Fruit
Whole Grain Toast	Corn Butter III	
Fruit Spreads	Herb Spread	
Fresh Fruit	Greens and Basil	
	Ice Cream	

BREAKFAST	DINNER	SUPPER

THURSDAY

BREAKFAST	DINNER	SUPPER
Fresh Pea Soup Whole Wheat Sesame Crackers Apple Crisp with Dessert Topping	Pita Bread with Falafels - Tomato, Mayonnaise, Sprouts, Green Onions, Olives Creamed Peas Peanut Butter Oaties	Carob Tofu Pie Crackers - Oatmeal-Barley with Olive Nut Filling Fresh Fruit

Friday

BREAKFAST	DINNER	SUPPER
Scrambled Tofu Pasta Casserole Whole Grain Bread - toasted Corn Butter & Fruit Jam Fresh Fruit	Baked Potato Avocado Topping or Gravy I Italian Olive Bread Corn Butter II Eggplant Super Tossed Salad with Italian Dressing	Pecan Bar

Saturday

BREAKFAST	DINNER	SUPPER
Fruit Pizza 6-8 Raw Almonds Fresh Fruit	Dill Caraway Potato Soup Greek Lentil Burgers Beet Salad with Orange Sauce Carrot Salad Whole Grain Bread with Creamy Cheese Spread Oatmeal-Carrot Cookies	Date Nut Strudel Orange Julius Fruit Salad Parfait

Sunday

BREAKFAST	DINNER	SUPPER
Grapefruit or Orange Rice Fruit Pudding Whole Grain Toast Fruit Jam Fresh Fruit	Cream of Onion Soup Vegie Burritos Corn Relish Tofu Cheese Cake	Raisin Muffins Peachy Fruit Shake Fresh Fruit

Monday

BREAKFAST	DINNER	SUPPER
Grapefruit or Orange Corn-Oat Waffles Banana Topping & Fruit Dressing Fresh Fruit	Lentil Roast Dilly Casserole Bread Corn Butter Potato Salad Sliced Cucumbers Cranberry Salad	Crepes with Tapioca Pudding and Strawberry Sauce Bread Sticks with Tofu-Avocado Dip Other Fresh Fruit

Tuesday

BREAKFAST	DINNER	SUPPER
Granola Strawberry Cream Toast & Almond Butter Fresh Fruit	Eggplant Delight Carrots a la Zucchini Oven "French Fried" Potatoes Bread & Corn Butter Carob Fudge	Cherry Soup Sweet Rolls Fresh Fruit

BREAKFAST	DINNER	SUPPER

Wednesday

French Toast Persimmon Whip Topping Fresh Fruit (2 kinds)	Tofu Stroganoff Tossed Salad (4 fresh items) Corn Bread Yeasty Spread Peanut Crunch Clusters	Date Nut Rolls Fresh Fruit Banana Ice Cream

Thursday

Legume Soup
Herbed Croutons
Sliced Tomatoes
Whole Grain Toast with
   Soy Mayonnaise
Fresh Peaches & Grapes
	Chick Peas a la King
	Salad Bar
	Bagels (served warm)
	Pinwheel-date-lemon Cookies
		Whole Grain Toast
		Pimiento Spread
		Corn Soup
		Cornbread Crackers
		   and Oatmeal Sticks
		Fresh Fruit

Friday

Millet Patties Country Gravy Sliced Tomatoes Sliced Cucumbers Whole Grain Toast Tofu Almond Spread	Cream of Tomato Soup Tabouli Salad Tomato-Spread Sandwich Pineapple-Coconut Dessert	Strawberry Jam on Whole Grain Bread Princess Pudding Peach Sauce Fresh Fruit

Saturday

Apricot-Pecan Wild Rice
Fresh Fruit
Whole Grain Toast
Fruit Jam
	South American
	   Dinner Menu
		Fruit Salad with Lime Dressing
		Rye Crackers &
		   3 Grain Crackers
		Toast - Jam

Sunday

Garbanzo French Toast Fruit Topping Fresh Fruit	Gazpacho Mexicali Casserole Mexican Corn Chowder Corn Tortillas Avocado Dip	Golden Fruit Soup Rye Crisp Banana Rolls - frozen

Monday

Black Beans & Rice
Chopped Avocado
Toast with Tomato &
   No Oil Mayonnaise
	Spaghetti with Sweet Red
	   Pepper Sauce
	Salad Bar
	French Bread with Garlic
	   Corn Butter
		Crackers with Grape Jam
		Whole Grain Toast with
		   Olive Spread
		Fresh Fruit

Tuesday

Sunflower Seed Waffles
Persimmon Whipped Topping
Fresh Fruit
	Chili
	Corn Bread
	   with Corn Spread
	Salad Bar
	Green Onion Dressing
		Fresh Pea Soup
		   (frozen)
		Crackers
		Fresh Fruit Pie

BREAKFAST	DINNER	SUPPER

Wednesday

Baked Oatmeal	Baked Potatoes with	Millet Soup
Pineapple Cream	Green Onion Dressing	Banana Crumble
Fresh Fruit	Herbed Lentil Loaf	Corn Crisps
Whole Grain Toast	Cabbage, Carrot, Radish	Fresh Fruit
	Salad	
	Lemon Juice with Seasonings	
	Bread with	
	Tofu Avocado Spread	
	Cookies	

Thursday

Fruit Toast	Holiday Loaf	Tomato Rice Soup
(hot fruit on whole	Baked Sweet Potatoes	Baked Apples
grain toast spread with	Green Beans	Crackers—Rye
almond butter)	Rolls & Corn Butter	Fresh Fruit
Fresh Fruit		

Friday

Scrambled Tofu	Lasagna with Pinto Beans	Rhubarb-Strawberry Cobbler
Hash Brown Potatoes	Salad Bar with Lettuce,	Summer Squash
Sliced Tomatoes	Radishes, Peas, Celery	or Zucchini Soup
Toast with Avocado	French Dressing	Jeanne's Crackers
	Coconut Macaroons	Fresh Fruit

Saturday

Delicious Millet	Black Beans & Rice	Popcorn
Fresh Fruit	Tossed Salad	Fruit Soup
Whole Grain Toast	Salsa	
Strawberry Jam	Melty Cheese	
	Pineapple Pie	

Check On Your Food Habits
Begin improving today — Check again in 2 weeks.

Now	2 Weeks later	

_____ _____ 1. I eat 2 or 3 regular meals each day.   (yes —————— 10 pts.)

_____ _____ 2. I eat at least 1 serving of dark green or yellow vegetables a day.
                                  (2 servings —————— 10 pts.)
                                  (1 serving —————— 5 pts.)

_____ _____ 3. I eat sparingly of nuts, avocadoes and olives.
                                  (2 servings —————— 5 pts.)
                                  (1 serving —————— 10 pts.)

_____ _____ 4. I eat a total of at least 3 servings of fruit each day with 1–2 fresh and raw.
                                  (2 servings —————— 10 pts.)
                                  (1 serving —————— 5 pts.)

_____ _____ 5. I eat a total of 2 or 3 servings of vegetables each day with 1-2 fresh and raw.
                                  (2 servings —————— 10 pts.)
                                  (1 serving —————— 5 pts.)

_____ _____ 6. I eat legumes such as soybeans, lentils, beans, peas, or garbanzos at least 2-3 times a week.
                                  (2-3 servings ——— 10 pts.)
                                  (1-2 servings ——— 5 pts.)

_____ _____ 7. Every day I eat whole grains in cereals and breads such as oatmeal, whole grain bread or toast, cooked wheat, rye, barley, millet, or others.
                                  (2-3 servings ——— 10 pts.)
                                  (1 - 2 servings ——— 5 pts.)

_____ _____ 8. I eat only small amounts of natural sweets and only with meals.
                                  (yes —————— 10 pts.)
                                  (sometimes —————— 5 pts.)

_____ _____ 9. I eat fresh, raw fruits or vegetables every meal.
                                  (yes —————— 5 pts.)

_____ _____ 10. I drink 6-8 glasses of water each day—between meals—rather than carbonated drinks or juice.   (yes —————— 5 pts.)

_____ _____ 11. I do not drink tea, coffee, or any caffeine drink.
                                  (yes —————— 5 pts.)

_____ _____ 12. I do not eat between meals and try to eat on schedule.
                                  (yes —————— 5pts.)

_____ _____ 13. I maintain a good emotional attitude at mealtime.
                                  (yes —————— 5 pts.)

_____ _____ 14. I do not rely on pills or drugs of any kind. (yes —————— 5 pts.)

Excellent— 100	Fair ———— 75 (Could use help)
Good ——— 90 (Keep working on it)	Poor ——— 74 and below (Need help)

Write or call Black Hills Health & Education Center, Box 19, Hermosa, SD 57744, 605-255-4101, or 255-4687

Breakfast Main Dishes

COOKING TIMES FOR GRAINS

Grain (1 c. dry)	Water:	Cooking Time:	Yield:
Barley (Whole)	3 cups	1 hour 15 minutes	3 ½ cups
Brown Rice	2 cups	1 hour	3 cups
Buckwheat (Kasha)	2 cups	15 minutes	2 ½ cups
Bulghur Wheat	2 cups	15-20 minutes	2 ½ cups
Cracked Wheat	2 cups	25 minutes	2 ⅓ cups
Millet	3 cups	45 minutes	3 ½ cups
Coarse Cornmeal (polenta)	4 cups	25 minutes	3 cups
Wild Rice	3 cups	1 hour or more	4 cups
Whole-Wheat Berries	3 cups	2 hours	2 ⅔ cups

Suggestions—Make Patties or Loaf from leftover cereal. Mix with vegies, onions, sprouts, oatmeal, garlic, sage, sweet basil, oregano. **Bake** ¾ hour at 350°.

CORN OAT WAFFLES

24	6	1 waffle servings
8 T.	2 T.	date sugar or 4 dates
12 c.	3 c.	oatmeal
2 c.	½ c.	cornmeal or millet flour
2 c.	½ c.	unsweetened coconut
2 t.	½ t.	salt

Cover with water. **Blend** thoroughly. Add water to make 22 cups total for large or 5 ½ cups total for small recipe. **Bake** 10 minutes in hot iron. **Cool** on rack.

CRUNCHY OKARA

Makes 3 qts.

6 c.	okara (see Index)
1 c.	peanuts or other nuts
1 c.	sesame seeds, ground fine
½ c.	carob powder
2 c.	date granules
3 c.	rolled oats
1 c.	sunflower seeds
1 c.	shredded coconut (macaroon)
1 t.	salt
1 T.	vanilla
1 t.	almond extract, pure

Mix all ingredients thoroughly. **Spread** mixture thinly on shallow pans. **Bake** 300° for 45 minutes, stirring at 10-15 minute intervals. May turn off oven and let dry out thoroughly.

This may be eaten by handfuls or served with soy milk as a breakfast food.

FRENCH TOAST - OVEN

25	5	1 slice servings
2 c.	⅓ c. + 1 T.	raw sesame seeds
15	3	dates
½ t.	dash	salt
5 c.	1 c.	water

Whiz. Dip (5) whole wheat bread slices in batter. **Broil** 450-500° on both sides until brown.

GARBANZO FRENCH TOAST

24	6	1 slice servings
4 c.	1 c.	soaked garbanzos
6 ⅔ c.	1 ⅔ c.	water
1 c.	¼ c.	cashews
2 t.	½ t.	salt
24	6	slices bread

Whiz. Dip bread in batter. Put on cookie sheet or Teflon® griddle. **Bake** until light brown.

GRANOLA

24	1 cup servings
14 c.	regular oats
2 ½ c.	whole wheat flour
2 c.	sunflower seeds
3 c.	coconut
1 ½ c.	sesame seeds, ground

In blender:

3 c.	dates
2 ½ c.	orange, pineapple or apple juice
3	bananas

Mix - crumble - bake 2 hours at 250°. **Stir. Watch** toward end of baking.

Add any or all of the following chopped.

1 c.	dried apricots, prunes
¾ c.	figs, raisins or other.

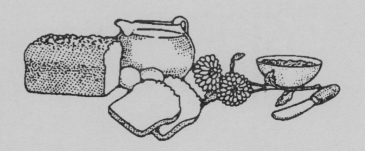

PANCAKES - OVEN

25	5	1 pancake servings
20	4	dates, pitted
1 ¼ c.	¼ c.	sesame seeds
12 ½ c.	2 ½ c.	water
7 ½ c.	1 ½ c.	rolled oats
2 ½ c.	½ c.	sunflower seeds
1-2 t.	½ t.	salt

Whiz all in blender. **Bake** on cookie sheets or crepe maker. Batter should be thinner for crepes.

SUNFLOWER SEED WAFFLES

24	3	1 waffle servings
20 c.	2 ½ c.	water
16 c.	2 c.	reg. rolled oats
4 c.	½ c.	sunflower seeds
2 c.	¼ c.	ground sesame seeds (measure before grinding)
½ c.	1 T.	date sugar or 2-3 dates
3 t.	½ t.	salt

Put all ingredients in blender and **blend** until smooth. **Bake** in medium hot waffle iron 8-10 minutes.

Do not open waffle iron until there is no more escaping steam.

(T) TOMATO TOAST

16	4	½ c. servings
8 c.	2 c.	tomatoes
¾ c.	3 T.	flour
¼ c.	1 T.	date sugar (optional)
4 c.	1 c.	tomato juice

Bring tomatoes to a **boil**. While they are heating, **blend** flour, date sugar, salt, and juice into a smooth paste. **Add** to boiling tomatoes and **stir** constantly until thickened. **Serve** over toast—for breakfast or supper.

WAFFLES, MULTI-GRAIN

30	10	servings
12 c.	4 c.	oatmeal
3 c.	1 c.	whole wheat flour
6 T.	2 T.	each of rye, barley, and soy flours
4 ½ t.	1 ½ t.	salt
1 ½ c.	½ c.	almonds or other nuts
6 T.	2 T.	sesame seeds

Blend dry in blender—**add** other dry ingredients and **mix** well.

¾ c.	¼-⅓ c.	dates
3 c.	1 c.	millet, cooked
15-18 c.	5-6 c.	hot water

Blenderize dates and millet in just enough of the hot water to blend well.

Add the above mixed dry ingredients and more of the water alternately as much as needed. Use more or less water to achieve desired thinness. **Bake** in hot waffle iron 8-12 minutes or until there is no escaping steam.

Suggestion: Make larger amount and freeze for further use.

WAFFLES, MULTI-GRAIN(no wheat)

30	10	1 waffle servings
14 c.	4 ½ c.	oatmeal
2 c.	⅔ c.	cashew nuts
¾ c.	¼ c.	sesame seeds
¾ c.	¼ c.	rye flour
1 ½ c.	½ c.	corn meal
12	4	dates
3 t.	1 t.	salt
3 c.	1 c.	soaked soybeans, raw (optional)
21–27 c.	7-9 c.	water or enough for easy pouring

Blenderize nuts, seeds, dates, soybeans and water. Add other ingredients and **mix** well. **Bake** in hot waffle iron 8-12 minutes or until there is no more escaping steam.

Idea — Try mashed pumpkin in pancakes or waffles:

	¾ t.	pumpkin pie seasoning
	½ c.	pecans
	½ c.	pumpkin

Crackers and Muffins
(no yeast)

BASIC INSTRUCTIONS: Blend water and nuts and seeds. **Add** to the dry ingredients. May need a little more water or flours to make soft dough. Flours vary in amount of water absorbed. **Prepare** all pans if not non-stick by using a small amount of lecithin (PAM) from non-aerosol bottle. **Spread** thin. May **add** cornmeal or bran which will fall off product when baked.

BREAD STICKS

24	4	Servings
3 c.	½ c.	coconut
3 c.	½ c.	ground nuts
12 c.	2 c.	flour (some non-wheat)
		wheat, barley, garbanzo, oatmeal
4 ½ c.	¾ c.	water

In blender, **blend** nuts smooth in the water. **Mix** well with the flours. **Roll** by hand into sticks 5" or 6" long, or roll dough out ¾" thick as for cookies and **cut** into ¾" strips 5" or 6" long. **Place** on baking sheet to **bake** at about 325° for 40 minutes—more or less.

CORN BREAD CRACKERS

24	12	Servings

In blender **combine:**

2 qt.	1 qt.	whole-kernel corn
4 c.	2 c.	water

Blend until smooth, then add:

1 c.	½ c.	ground sesame seeds

Blend again. **Pour** into bowl and **stir** in:

2 c.	1 c.	corn meal
1 t.	½ t.	salt
½ t.	¼ t.	coriander
1 t.	½ t.	onion powder

Pour onto baking sheet. **Bake** at 350° for 40 minutes or until crisp on top.

CRACKERS - 3 GRAIN

24	6	Servings
6 c.	1 ½ c.	flour
4 c.	1 c.	oat flour
6 c.	1 ½ c.	fine cornmeal
2 t.	½ t.	salt
1 ⅓ c.	⅓ c.	walnuts
1 ⅓ c.	⅓ c.	ground sesame seeds
6 c.	1 ½ c.	Water for cracker consistency

Blenderize water and nuts until smooth. **Mix** well with rest of ingredients. **Roll** out thin on nonstick cookie sheet. **Bake** at 350° for 10 minutes or more. **Watch!**

CRACKERS OR PIE CRUST

12	3	Pie crusts
24	6	Cracker servings
4 c.	1 c.	oat flour or quick oats, ground
6 c.	1 ½ c.	rice or barley flour
6 c.	1 ½ c.	fine cornmeal (for crackers)
1 ⅓ c.	⅓ c.	sesame or sunflower seeds, ground
1 ⅓ c.	⅓ c.	walnuts
6 c.	1 ½ c.	water, scant

Blenderize nuts and seeds in the water. **Mix** with other ingredients. **Roll** out on cookie sheet. **Sprinkle** with a little salt or garlic powder and cut. **Bake** at 250° until crunchy. **Roll** out between Handy-Wrap® for pie crust.

CRACKERS - WHOLE WHEAT

24	4	Servings
3 c.	½ c.	nuts, ground fine
4 ½ c.	¾ c.	water
3 t.	½ t.	salt
9 c.	1 ½ c.	whole wheat flour

Blenderize nuts in the water. **Add** flour and salt. **Roll** out and **turn** several times. **Roll** very thin. **Bake** at 350° 15-20 minutes.

CRACKERS - WHOLE WHEAT SESAME

24	4	Servings
4 ½ c.	¾ c.	water
1 ½ t.	¼ t.	salt
9 c.	1 ½ c.	whole wheat flour
3 c.	½ c.	sesame seeds

Method—same as Whole Wheat Crackers.

OATMEAL STICKS

24	4	Servings
4 c.	⅔ c.	water
2 T.	1 t.	vanilla
12 c.	2 c.	oatmeal
3 c.	½ c.	cashews
1 ½ c.	¼ c.	date sugar
5-6 c.	¾-1 c.	whole wheat flour
2 T.	1 t.	salt

Place water, vanilla, date sugar and cashews in blender and **blend** well. In a bowl, **put** all ingredients and **mix** lightly. **Knead** a smooth ball, **divide** and **roll** out on 2 cookie sheets. **Bake** 20-25 minutes at 350° until light brown.

ONION POTATO CRISPS

24	4	¼ c. servings
12 T.	2 T.	dried onion flakes
2 T.	1 t.	poppy seeds
6 c.	1 c.	cooked potatoes

POTATO CRISPS

24	4	¼ c. servings - 4 Crisps
6 c.	1 c.	cooked, mashed potatoes
3 t.	½ t.	caraway seed
		Salt to taste

SWEET CRISPS

24	2	½ c. servings
3 c.	¼ c.	coconut shreds
12 c.	1 c.	rice

Roll out on floured table. **Cut** in rounds and **place** on cookie sheet. **Re-roll** until all made up. **Bake** at 350° 25-30 minutes.

SESAME STICKS

24	4	Servings
9 c.	1 ½ c.	whole wheat flour
3 c.	½ c.	soy flour
6 T.	1 T.	date sugar (or 3 dates blended in the water)
2 c.	⅓ c.	sesame seeds
3 t.	½ t.	salt
2 c.	⅓ c.	walnuts (ground to paste in nut grinder)
4 ½ c.	¾ c.	cold water

In a bowl **mix** whole wheat flour, soy flour, date sugar and salt. In blender **put** water, sesame seeds and walnuts, and **blend** smooth. **Mix** well with other ingredients. **Roll** into strips about ½" around and cut into 3" sticks. **Bake** at 350° about ½ hour or until golden brown.

WHOLE WHEAT OAT STICKS

24	4	Servings
12 c.	2 c.	whole wheat flour
12 c.	2 c.	oat flour or ground oats
6 c.	1 c.	ground almonds
6 t.	1 t.	salt
12 c.	2 c.	dates, chopped
2 c.	⅓ c.	coconut
6 c.	1 c.	water

Combine dry ingredients and dates in a bowl. **Blenderize** the water, coconut and almonds. **Add** water mix to dry ingredients and **stir** into a stiff dough. **Add** more water if necessary. **Knead** only enough to form a dough ball. **Divide** dough and **roll** out onto 2 large prepared cookie sheets to ¼"-⅛" thickness. **Prick** with a fork and **cut** into strips ¾" by 3" **Bake** at 400° until brown on top and bottom. **Turn** if necessary. **Watch** edges! **Remove** when brown.

Sauces & Syrups
Toppings & Frostings

ALMOND ICING

(Amounts of finished product are approximate.)
Makes 2 cups

Blend thoroughly:
1 c.	coconut
1 c.	water
2	dried pineapple rings

Add:
⅔ c.	cooked millet (soft)
1 t.	almond extract

Blend until smooth. **Add** more water if necessary for icing consistency.
Serve on rolls, fruit salad, fruits, or desserts.

BANANA TOPPING

Makes 1 cup

Peel 2 very ripe bananas. **Freeze** in plastic bag. **Slice** bananas in a blender with a small amount of cashew milk, approximately ⅓ cup, and this will make a thick mixture like whipping cream. **Add** a very small amount of lemon juice to keep bananas from turning brown.

CAROB DATE SYRUP

48	*1 T. Servings (3 cups)*
2 c.	water
2 c.	soft dates (Check dates— be sure no pits!)
½ c.	carob powder

Blend until smooth. **Pour** into quart glass jar and add 1 c. water (use this to rinse out the blender). **Stir** well.
Add 5 T. syrup to 1 c. water to make a delicious hot or cold drink or **mix** ½ c. rice milk with ½ c. water and **add** 4 T. carob syrup. **Blend** until smooth.
Also use as you would chocolate syrup.
Delicious on bananas with chopped nuts sprinkled on top.

CAROB FROSTING

Makes 2 ½ cups

⅓ c.	almonds
2 c.	water
pinch	salt
15	dates
4 t.	oatmeal
2-3 T.	carob

Blend until smooth. **Cook** to thicken. **Add:**
½ c.	coconut or nuts
¼ t.	almond flavoring
1 t.	vanilla

COCONUT FROSTING

Makes 1 cup

1 c.	water
¾ c.	coconut
1 T.	cornstarch
3 T.	apple juice concentrate
¼ t.	salt
½ t.	natural flavoring (lemon, almond, orange, pineapple— your choice)

Blend until smooth. **Cook** to thicken. **Stir** constantly. Cool.

CREAMY TOPPING

Makes 1 cup

1 ½ c.	tofu
2 T.	frozen fruit juice concentrate (your choice or to taste)
	Drop or two of fresh lemon juice

Blend until smooth. **Serve** on fruit, cobblers, crisps, etc.

- 27 -

DESSERT TOPPING

Makes 4 cups

1 c.	water
1/3 c.	dates
1/3 c.	dried pineapple
1/4 t.	salt
1 t.	vanilla
2 1/2 c.	soybean base (see Index)
3 T.	macaroon coconut
1/4 c.	cashew nuts
1/4 t.	lemon juice
1/4 t.	orange juice

Thoroughly **blenderize** all ingredients until very smooth. **Chill** before using.

FRUIT DRESSING

Makes 2 cups

1 c.	No Oil Soy Mayonnaise (see Index)
1	crushed banana(s)
1/2 c.	crushed pineapple, unsweetened
1/4 c.	fresh coconut

Blenderize thoroughly. **Use** on any fruit salad.

PERSIMMON WHIPPED TOPPING

Makes 1 cup

1	medium persimmon
2 T.	orange juice concentrate
1/2 c.	tofu

Blend. Nice topping for desserts.

PINEAPPLE ORANGE TOPPING

Makes 1 qt.

1/2 c.	cashew nuts
12 oz.	can pineapple-orange concentrate
12 oz.	water
1	golden delicious apple, peeled and cored
2 T.	arrowroot or corn starch

Blend well. **Simmer** to thicken. Topping for fruit, cobblers, etc.

RHUBARB TOPPING for crisps

Makes 3 cups

4 c.	(about 1 1/2 pounds) trimmed rhubarb stalks, cut into 1" pieces
3/4 c.	date sugar
	grated zest of 1 orange
1/2 c.	berry concentrate
1 c.	sliced strawberries

Toss rhubarb with date sugar, orange zest and juice in large mixing bowl. **Cover** and **marinate** 30 minutes. **Transfer** to large saucepan and **cook** over low heat until rhubarb is very tender but keeps its shape. **Add** strawberries and **simmer** 5 minutes. Transfer to bowl, **cover** with plastic wrap and **chill**. Serve with a scoop of Pineapple Ice Cream (see *Cooking With Natural Foods* - first book) or with granola.

STRAWBERRY TOPPING for crepes

Makes 5 cups

12 oz.	water
1-12 oz.	can Tree Top Fruit N Berry conc.
3 T.	tapioca
3 T.	cornstarch mixed with 1/3 c. juice
1 lb.	frozen whole strawberries, unsweetened

Bring water and juice concentrate to a **boil**. **Stir** into juice/cornstarch mix. **Cook** until thick and clear. **Pour** over sliced berries. **Stir** carefully. May add a little more water if thinner sauce is wanted. Good over crepes or Tofu Cheesecake too.

(A good filling for crepes is the Fruit Braid Spread recipe on p. 92 of *Cooking With Natural Foods*. An electric crepe maker is the best way to make perfect crepes. Very special for banquets, etc.)

WHIPPED TOPPING

Makes 2 1/2 cups

2 c.	pineapple juice
1/2 c.	millet

Cook *really* soft. **Blend** to cool. **Add** vanilla to taste. May need to add some dried pineapple to make it sweet enough. **Blend** well again after adding.

MILKS AND CREAMS

The variety of milks and creams that can be made are limitless! Grains can be used, nuts, fruits—fresh, canned or dried. **Blend** well for smooth milks. If you wish to thicken the milk (cream), **add** more nuts or use dried fruit (dried apples will blend with most fruits). Soy milk blends well with fruits also.

ALMOND FRUIT MILK

32	8	½ cup servings
2 c.	½ c.	almonds
2 c.	½ c.	dried apples
½ t.	⅛ t.	salt
16 c.	4 c.	water

Grind almonds in blender. **Simmer** apples in 1 c. water until soft. **Put** salt, almonds, apples and water and 1 more cup water in blender. **Blend** until very smooth. **Pour** into container, **add** rest of water (2 c.)—this can be used to rinse out blender before adding. **Stir** well before serving. Cashews can be used in place of almonds and any dried fruit in place of the apples.

MILLET MILK

Cook very soft:

⅔ c.	hot millet
½ c.	almonds
1 t.	vanilla
1 t.	salt
1 T.	date sugar or dried pineapple
3 c.	water

Blend smooth.

PINEAPPLE CREAM

18	9	⅓ c. servings

Blend the following until smooth:

2 c.	1 c.	cashews
4 c.	2 c.	pineapple juice
4	2	apples—golden delicious
3 T.	1 ½ T.	arrowroot
¼ t.	⅛ t.	salt

Cook over low heat until thick, **stirring** constantly. **Cool.** Orange juice (in place of pineapple) makes a delicious variation.

RICE CREAM TOPPING

24	8	2 T. servings
3 c.	1 c.	cooked brown rice (well done, soft and still warm)
½ c.	⅙ c.	cashews
3 T.	1 T.	vanilla
½-¾ c.	2-4 T.	chopped, dried pineapple
¾ t.	¼ t.	salt

Blend until very creamy **adding** just enough water to keep a whipped cream-like consistency. **Place** in refrigerator and **chill** until cold.

SOY MILK OR CREAM

32	16	½ c. servings
2 c.	1 c.	soybean base
6	2-3	dates
1 t.	½ t.	vanilla
	pinch	salt

Add water or ice cubes to make 4 or 2 quarts, depending on recipe size. **Blend** thoroughly. For cream, use less water.

BREADS (yeast)

Notice

Bread making can be a very rewarding experience. When considering a recipe, check the amount of liquid. Usually 1 c. of water will make a 1 lb. loaf. When making rolls or bagels, the size of the product will determine the count.

All bread recipes can be made in a bread maker. For most bread, when using a bread maker, all of the ingredients may be put in the bowl. Then add flour until the dough leaves the sides of the bowl. Let the machine knead the bread for about 10 minutes and proceed with loaves, rolls, bread stix, etc.

BAGELS OR DINNER ROLLS

These rolls are very flavorful. When shaping them, push your thumb through the middle of each piece of dough and shape into bagels instead of dinner rolls.

Blend until smooth 3 c. warm water with 1 c. cooked squash or pumpkin.

Pour into large bowl or mixer.

Blend 3 c. warm water with 2 c. raisins until raisins are chunky. **Add** to squash mixture.

Blend in 4 T. yeast. Let **set** 5 minutes.

Add whole wheat flour while **beating** to cake batter consistency. Continue to beat while **adding**:

½ c.	ground sesame seeds
2 T.	salt
1 T.	cardamon
½ c.	gluten flour
¾ c.	quick oats

Beat 5 minutes more. **Cover**. Let **rest** until double in bulk. **Beat** again while adding just enough flour (all whole wheat or part golden) until dough does not stick to fingers. Be careful not to add too much flour. **Shape** into rolls or bagels. Let **double** in size under a towel in pans or on cookie sheets.

Bake at 375°. About 30 minutes for pans of rolls. About 20 minutes for individual buns or bagels.

BAGELS-ONION

6 T.	2 T.	yeast
12 c.	3 ¾ c.	whole wheat flour
4 ½ c.	1 ½ c.	lukewarm water
9 T.	3 T.	date sugar
1 ½ t.	½ t.	salt
1 ½	½	chopped onion, optional
3 T.	1 T.	chives
	pinch	sweet basil or any salad herb

Combine yeast and 3 c. flour. **Combine** water, date sugar, salt, yeast. **Beat** at low speed for ½ minutes. **Add** remaining ingredients. **Beat** 3 minutes at high speed. **Add** enough more flour to make dough moderately stiff. **Knead** 5-8 minutes. Let **rise** 15 minutes. **Cut** into 12 portions. **Shape** into smooth balls. **Punch** a hole with floured finger into center. **Pull** gently to enlarge hole. **Cover**. Let **rise** 20 minutes. Bring 1 gallon water and 1 T. date sugar to **boil**. Reduce to **simmer**. **Drop** bagels into water 4 at a time for 7 minutes, turning once. **Drain**. **Place** on cookie sheet. **Bake** 35 minutes at 375°.

Basic whole-wheat bread

BREAD-HERB

4	2	loaves
1 c.	½ c.	minced onion
1 c.	½ c.	nuts and seeds
3 c.	1 ½ c.	water
1 c.	½ c.	snipped parsley (1 T. dried)
4 T.	2 T.	dates or apple sauce
4 t.	2 t.	salt
1 t.	½ t.	dried dill weed, or
4 t.	2 t.	chopped fresh dill
½ t.	¼ t.	ground sage
4 T.	2 T.	dry yeast
1 c.	½ c.	warm water
		date sugar or malt
8 c.	4 c.	whole wheat flour, preferably stone ground or part whole wheat and part golden flour
1 ½ c.	¾ c.	cornmeal, freshly ground

In a large mixing bowl **combine** the yeast, warm water, and dates or apple sauce. When bubbly, **add** the water and seasonings. **Add** 2 ½ c. flour and **beat** 2 minutes with an electric mixer or at least 200 strokes by hand. **Add** the cornmeal and **mix** thoroughly. Gradually **add** about 1 ½ c. more flour, or enough to form a dough that clings together and pulls away from the sides of the bowl.

Turn the dough out onto a floured surface and **knead** until smooth and elastic, **sprinkling** with a little more flour if it remains too sticky. **Cover** with a damp towel and let **rise** until doubled. **Punch down** and **divide** into 2 balls. **Sprinkle** a baking sheet with cornmeal. **Make** round loaves and **place** on the baking sheet. You may want to **slash** a cross in the tops with a sharp knife. **Cover** the loaves with a damp towel and let **rise** until almost doubled in bulk.

Preheat the oven to 350°. **Bake** about 45 minutes, or until the bottoms sound hollow when thumped. **Remove** from pans to cool on a rack.

BREAD-NO KNEAD

½ t.	salt	
6 c.	whole wheat flour	
2	pkg. yeast	
1 c.	warm water	
2 c.	hot water	
2	apples	

Dissolve yeast in warm water. **Blend** hot water and apples. **Stir** together and **spoon** into pans. Let **rise** 15 minutes. **Preheat** oven to 400°. **Bake** 30 minutes at 350°.

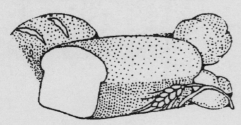

BREAD-SPECIAL

1 c.	mashed potatoes or squash
1 c.	water or potato water
1 c.	nuts, ground fine
⅓ c.	dates
1 ½ t.	salt
¼ c.	warm water
1 ½ T.	yeast
½ t.	date sugar
6 ½ c.	golden flour

Combine as for bread. **Roll** or **pat** out to fit large shallow casserole or use 3 pie dishes. Let **rise** almost double. Indent with thumb and fill with topping.

Topping: Tofu, date sugar, coriander, cooked-dried apricots, raisins, prunes.

Bake at 400° 15-20 minutes or until golden brown. **Serve** warm the second day.

BREAD-WHOLE WHEAT

5	loaves

Blend very well:

2 c.	very warm water
½ c.	raisins
1 ½ T.	yeast
½ c.	sunflower seeds, ground
1-250	mg. Vitamin C, or
1 T.	lemon juice for each 2 ½ c. flour
1 T.	salt
2 c.	water
7-10 c.	whole wheat flour
½ c.	golden flour

Knead 10 minutes in bread maker. Slowly **add** flour to right consistency—it will begin to leave side of bowl. **Proceed** as usual.

CORN BREAD

36	12	3" x 3" servings

Mix and set aside:

6 c.	2 c.	cornmeal
3 c.	1 c.	quick oats
1 ½ c.	½ c.	whole wheat flour
1 ½ c.	½ c.	golden flour
3 t.	1 t.	salt

In another bowl **mix**:

3 c.	1 c.	apple sauce
6 c.	2 c.	hot water
3 T.	1 T.	yeast

Mix all together. **Place** in prepared 9" x 12" pan. Let **rise** 30 minutes. **Bake** at 350° for 30 minutes.

CORN MEAL WHEAT ROLLS OR BUNS

60	30	1/3 c. rolls or buns
3 c.	1 ½ c.	cold water
5 c.	2 ½ c.	cornmeal
3 t.	1 ½ t.	salt
7 c.	3 ½ c.	boiling water
4 c.	2 c.	very warm water
¼ c.	2 T.	diastatic malt or
6 T.	3 T.	date sugar
6 T.	3 T.	yeast

Stir corn meal and salt into cold water, then into boiling water. Bring to **boil**. **Remove** from heat and let **set** 15-20 minutes, uncovered. **Mix** yeast and malt in 2 c. very warm water. Let **set** 5 minutes. **Put** yeast mixture and 4 c. whole wheat flour in large bowl and **mix** well with electric mixer 2-3 minutes until very elastic. **Add** corn meal mixture and 4 more cups whole wheat flour. **Mix** vigorously until well blended and let **rise** until double. For rolls, **fill** prepared muffin tins ⅔ full and let **rise** to top. For buns, spoon onto prepared cookie sheet like large patties. Let **rise**. **Bake** at 350° about ½ hour or until done.

DATE NUT FILLING for strudel

36	12	small servings
6 c.	2 c.	dates (and enough water to cook and blend)
3 c.	1 c.	almonds, ground fine
3 c.	1 c.	walnuts or pecans, ground fine
1 ½-3 t.	½-1 t.	anise seed (to taste)
3 t.	1 t.	vanilla
9 T.	3 T.	carob powder
6 T.	2 T.	Pero
6 T.	2 T.	grated orange peel
1 ½ c.	½ c.	soy powder, opt.
2 ¼ c.	¾ c.	carob chips, opt.

Mix everything together. **Spread** on dough. **Bake** at 350° for 35-40 minutes.

DATE NUT ROLLS

Use recipe for bagels or dinner rolls.
Filling:

1 ½ c.	pitted dates
¾ c.	chopped nuts
1 t.	lemon juice
1 ½ c.	water

Boil dates until soft. **Mash** smooth. **Add** nuts. **Spread** on bread dough and **roll** as jelly roll. **Cut** ½" wide and **place** on prepared cookie sheet. Let **rise**. **Bake** at 375° for 20-25 minutes.

DATE NUT STRUDEL

36	12	small servings
12 c.	4 c.	flour (½ whole wheat, ½ golden)
¾ c.	¼ c.	ground almonds
6 T.	2 T.	soy flour
3 T.	1 T.	lemon peel
1 ½ c.	½ c.	soy powder
3 c..	1 c.	lukewarm water
4 ½ T.	1 ½ T.	yeast
2 T.	1 T.	date sugar

Mix as usual for bread.

Let **rise** once. **Roll** dough on large floured tea towel with rolling pin. **Spread** filling over dough. **Roll** like jelly roll, then **put** carefully on cookie sheet. **Shape** into horse shoe. **Slit** at 1 inch intervals then **turn** each section. If desired, decorate with sliced almonds and cherries.

DILLY CASSEROLE BREAD

24	8	servings
3	1	package(s) active dry yeast
¾ c.	¼ c.	very warm water (105° to 115°F)
3 c.	1 c.	tofu
6 T.	2 T.	date sugar
3 T.	1 T.	instant minced onion
6 t.	2 t.	dill seed
3 t.	1 t.	salt
3 T.	1 T.	nut butter
7 ½ c.	2 ½ c.	golden or unbleached flour

In large bowl, **soften** yeast in warm water. In small saucepan, **heat** tofu to lukewarm. **Combine** tofu, date sugar, onion, dill seed, 1 t. salt and yeast. Lightly **spoon** flour into measuring cup; **level** off; **add** 1 ½ c. flour. **Beat** for 2 minutes at medium speed. By hand, **stir in** remaining 1 c. flour. **Mix** thoroughly. **Cover**; let **rise** in warm place until light and doubled in size, 50-60 minutes.

Prepare an 8-inch round 1 ½ or 2 quart casserole with lecithin. **Stir** down dough; **turn** into casserole. Let **rise** in warm place until light and doubled in size, 30-40 minutes. **Heat** oven to 350°. **Bake** for 40-50 minutes, until golden brown. Immediately **remove** from pan and **spray** with salt water.

FOUR GRAIN POTATO BREAD

6-8	loaves
1/3 c.	active dry yeast
4 c.	whole wheat flour
2 c.	rye flour
1 1/2 c.	cornmeal
3 c.	golden flour (has germ and some bran)
6 c.	nut milk (6 c. water with 1 c. nuts blended)
1 c.	dates, soft
1 c.	uncooked quick-cooking oatmeal
2 T.	salt
1-1 1/2 c.	cooked, mashed squash or potatoes
9-12 c.	whole wheat flour

Combine first six ingredients in a large bowl; **Mix. Combine** remaining ingredients, except the 9-12 cups flour, in a large saucepan, **stirring** to mix well. **Heat** until mixture reaches 110° to 115°F. **Pour** warm liquid into dry ingredients. **Stir** well 3-4 minutes. **Add** remaining flour, 1 cup at a time, **mixing** well after each addition, until dough leaves side of bowl. **Turn** onto lightly-floured board and **knead** 5-7 minutes. Let double in bulk. **Punch** down. **Shape** and **place** in prepared bread pans. Let **rise** until double in bulk. **Preheat** oven to 350°. **Bake** loaves 35-40 minutes.

ITALIAN OLIVE BREAD

24	8	servings
15 c.	5 c.	flour
6 pkg.	2 pkg.	yeast
1/2 c.	3 T.	date sugar
2 t.	1 t.	salt
3 c.	1 c.	warm water
3 c.	1 c.	pimientos or sautéed red peppers
4 1/2 c.	1/2 c.	green pitted olives

Make a soft bread dough with the first five ingredients. **Drain** olives and **pat dry** in paper towels. Pulse **chop** 3-4 times. **Cut** dough in 4 pieces and **roll** out to 1/2". **Spread** 1/4 of the olives and pimentos over dough and **press** in lightly. **Roll** up as jelly roll. **Place** seam side down on prepared baking sheet sprinkled with cornmeal. Let **rise** 25 minutes. **Bake** at 350° 40-45 minutes. **Slice** in 1" widths. **Serve** warm.

KASHA BREAD

9	3	loaves
3 c.	1 c.	raisins
4 1/2 c.	1 1/2 c.	water

Blend above to make paste. **Add** water to make 2 1/2 c.

6 T.	2 T.	ground nuts
6 t.	2 t.	yeast
1 1/2 c.	1/2 c.	water
3/4 c.	1/4 c.	buckwheat groats (rinse, drain, dextrinize) (turns reddish and smells good)
5 t.	2 t.	salt
17 c.	5 1/2 c.	whole wheat flour

Form in ball and let **rise** 1 1/2 hours or less. If hole doesn't fill in when dented take next step. **Press** flat. **Make** smooth round and let **rise** (takes 1/2 as long as the first time). **Divide** in 2—handle gently. **Make** round loaves. **Cover** so they don't dry out. Let **rise** 30-45 minutes until dent fills in slowly. **Bake** at 400° for 10 minutes then 350° for 50 minutes or more.

MILLET BREAD

27	9	3" x 3" servings
7 1/2 c.	2 1/2 c.	water
6 T.	2 T.	dry yeast
3	1	apple
6 t.	2 t.	salt
3 c.	1 c.	millet flour
6 c.	2 c.	cornmeal
6 c.	2 c.	oat flour
7 1/2 c.	2 1/2 c.	sunflower seeds, ground

Mix well. **Pour** into pan 9" x 9". **Rise** 40 minutes or until increased one-half. **Bake** at 350° 45 minutes until brown.

MUFFINS-DATE, APPLE SAUCE

Dissolve 2 T. yeast and 1 T. date crystals in 1/2 c. warm water. Set aside, let **foam**.

Meanwhile, **whiz**:

1 c.	warm water
1-1 1/2 c.	dates
1 t.	vanilla
1 c.	applesauce
1/2 c.	whole wheat flour
1 t.	salt

Add to above the yeast mixture. Stir as little as possible. Then **fold** in one more cup whole wheat flour. Set aside to **rise** 15-20 minutes, not more. **Fold in** 1 3/4 c. more flour. **Put** in muffin tins. Let **set** 5-6 minutes, not more. **Bake** at 350° for 30 minutes.

MULTI GRAIN BREAD

24	8	1 lb. loaves
3 c.	1 c.	ground sunflower or sesame seeds
6 qts.	8 c.	very warm water
4 ½ c.	1 ½ c.	apple sauce or
		cooked potato puree or squash puree
¾ c.	4 T.	bread yeast
3 c..	1 c.	gluten flour
1 ½ c.	½ c.	oatmeal
¾ c.	¼ c.	millet
¾ c.	¼ c.	cornmeal
¾ c.	¼ c.	rye flakes
1 ½ t.	½ t.	ascorbic acid powder or
3 T.	1 T.	lemon juice

Add whole wheat flour to the above in breadmaker to make a cake batter consistency. **Beat** at low speed for 8 minutes. Let **rise** until double in bulk. **Add** 2 T. salt and enough whole wheat flour to make bread dough consistency. **Add** this flour slowly as you don't want to get too much flour in your dough or it will be tough. When dough pulls away from sides of bowl and is just barely not sticky it is just right. Let **rise** until double again. **Punch down** and **mold** into loaves, rolls, bread sticks, etc. Let **rise** until double. **Bake** in preheated 350° oven 45-60 minutes for bread loaves, 20-30 minutes for dinner rolls, 10-15 minutes for bread sticks. **Remove** from pans and **cool** before storing.

MULTI GRAIN BREAD VARIATION

10	5	1 lb. loaves
10 c.	5 c.	warm water
1 ½ c.	¾ c.	cooking dates, squash or potato

Liquefy dates in water.

8 c.	4 c.	whole wheat flour
4 T.	2 T.	dry yeast

Combine warm water and dates, 4 c. whole wheat flour and yeast in mixing bowl. Let **rest** 5-10 minutes. Then **add:**

½ c.	¼ c.	cashew meal(any nuts or seeds,
		ground fine)
2 T.	1 T.	salt

Mix. Then **add:**

6 c.	3 c.	whole wheat flour
1 ½ c.	¾ c.	gluten flour
1 c.	½ c.	barley flour
1 c.	½ c.	oatmeal flour
1 c.	½ c.	cornmeal (whole grind)
1 c.	½ c.	soy flour
1 c.	½ c.	rye flour

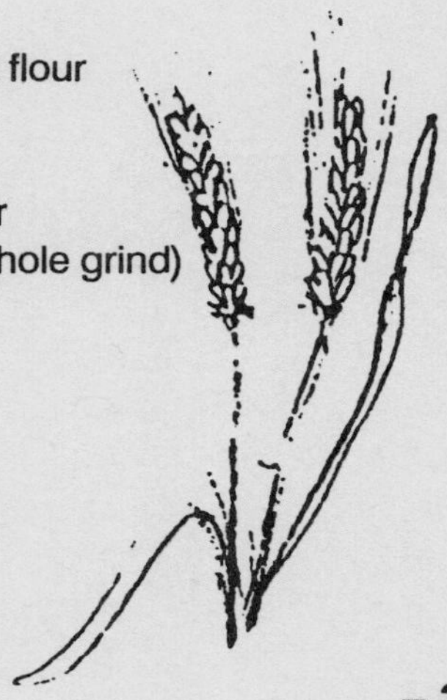

Add flours until dough begins to pull away from the side of the mixing bowl. **Knead** for 10 minutes. **Remove** dough from mixer. **Place** on floured surface. **Divide** and **form** into loaves. **Place** loaves in Silverstone-coated or Pam-sprayed bread pans. **Cover** loaves with a damp cloth and let **rise** until almost double in bulk.

Bake at 350° for 45-60 minutes. **Remove** bread from pans and **place** on a rack to cool.

PITA BREAD

60	15	pitas
4	1	package(s) yeast (1 T.)
5 c.	1 ¼ c.	warm water
4 t.	1 t.	date sugar
14 c.	3 ½ c.	or more whole wheat flour
2 t.	½ t.	salt
4 T.	1 T.	ground sunflower or sesame seeds

Make dough until smooth and elastic—no longer sticky. Let **rise** double in covered bowl. **Punch down**. **Knead** lightly. **Divide** into balls size of small orange. Let dough **rest** to relax dough. **Roll** out circle to ½" thick. **Sift** lightly each circle with flour. **Cover** with wax paper.

Heat oven until very hot (450° or more). **Prepare** 2 baking sheets (lightly sprayed with Pam). **Spray** lightly with water the circles of dough. **Place** on baking sheets and put in hot oven. Pitas will puff up. **Bake** 6-8 minutes. **Bake** until soft and not browned. **Remove** to cooling racks.

RAISIN MUFFINS

3 c.	1 c.	hot water
9 c.	3 c.	regular oatmeal
1 ½ c.	½ c.	full fat soy flour
3 c.	1 c.	whole wheat flour
1 c.	⅓ c.	sesame seeds (ground)
2 c.	⅔ c.	raisins
1 ½ t.	½ t.	salt
3 c.	1 c.	golden flour

Mix all dry ingredients and ⅓ c. raisins. **Put** ground sesame seeds and ⅓ c. raisins in 1 c. hot water and **blend** well. **Add** needed liquid to dry ingredients and **mix** well. Use ice cream scoop to put into prepared muffin pans. **Let stand** 5-10 minutes. (Each muffin should be about 1" thick.) **Bake** at 350°-375° until lightly browned—about ½ hour.

RYE BISCUITS

3	1	loaf (loaves)
3 c.	1 c.	lukewarm potato water
1 ½	½	cake(s) compressed yeast
3 t.	1 t.	date sugar
	pinch	sea salt
3 c.	1 c.	whole wheat bread flour

Blend ingredients and make into a sponge. Let **rise** until foamy, about 1 hour. Then work briskly and **add** the following:

2 t.	1 t.	caraway seeds, opt.
1 t.	½ t.	anise seeds, opt.
3 c.	1 c.	sunflower seeds, ground
4 ½ c.	1 ½ c.	rye flour, enough to make a hard loaf

Let **rise** until double. **Bake** 30 minutes at 350°.

SESAME MUFFINS

27	9	big muffins
3 c.	1 c.	lukewarm potato water
1 ½	½	cake(s) compressed yeast
3 T.	1 T.	date sugar or dates

Dissolve yeast, **add** dates and let **rise** for 10 minutes. **Add**:

⅛ t.	pinch	sea salt
¾ c.	4 T.	sunflower seeds, ground
3 T.	1 T.	cracked wheat or bulghur
5 ¼ c.	1 ¾ c.	whole grain bread flour
1 c.	½ c.	sesame seeds, ground

Mix ingredients and **pour** batter in well-greased muffin tins. Let **rise** while oven heats, **bake** about 25 minutes, or until done, in a 400° oven. You can vary with chopped sunflower seeds.

SQUASH ROLLS

18 c.	6 ½ c.	flour (or more)
4	2	pakages yeast
1 ½ c.	½ c.	apple sauce
6 ¾ c.	1 ¼ c.	squash
6 c.	2 c.	warm water
3 T.	1 T.	orange peel

Mix all in bread maker for 10 minutes. May need more flour to make non-sticky dough. Use for dinner rolls, sweet rolls, cobbler or fruit pizza. **Bake** 30 minutes at 350°.

THREE SEED BREAD

4	loaves
1 c.	very hot water
½ c.	date crystals

Let set to soften. **Blend**. **Add** 3 c. warm water and place in mixing bowl with the following:

1 t.	salt
1 ½ c.	oatmeal or oat flour
1 c.	sunflower seeds
½ c.	sesame seeds, ground
¼ c.	poppy seeds
2 t.	yeast
6-8 c.	whole wheat flour

Knead in bread maker for ten minutes. **Make** into loaves. **Let rise** and **bake** until well done. 350° for 45-60 minutes.

Note: Any bread recipe may be made in a bread maker or by hand.

Main Dishes

APRICOT PECAN WILD RICE

24	12	½ c. servings
2 lb.	1 lb.	Wild Rice or "Lundberg" Wild Blend (soaked in cold water overnight)
4 c.	2 c.	vegetable broth and/or chicken-like seasoned broth
2 ⅔ c.	1 ⅓ c.	toasted chopped pecans
1 ⅓ c.	⅔ c.	chopped dried apricots (¼ lb.)
½ c.	¼ c.	raisins
½ c.	¼ c.	orange juice concentrate
1 t.	½ t.	cinnamon substitute (see Index)
1 t.	½ t.	sage leaf, crumbled

Bake at 350° 45-60 minutes or until rice is cooked.

BAKED TOFU

24	12	½ cup servings
8 c.	4 c.	whole grain bread cubes
4 c.	2 c.	tofu, cubed
4 t.	2 t.	chicken-style seasoning (see Index)
4-6 c.	2-3 c.	soy or nut milk

Layer bread, then tofu. **Sprinkle** with seasoning. **Add** the milk to cover. **Bake** 30-45 minutes or until brown.

This dish is very versatile as it can be seasoned with onion, garlic, sage, rosemary, oregano; **add** tomato pieces, eggplant, summer squash, frozen peas, green beans. Or it can be made for a fruit meal by using date sugar, pieces of fruit such as peaches, apricots, apples, plums, etc.

Be creative - use your ingenuity!

BEAN AND WALNUT CASSEROLE

24	8	½ c. servings

From Russia—Walnuts are crushed with garlic and used in many of their dishes including eggplant and soups.

4 ½ c.	1 ½ c.	dried beans (any kind except limas)
6	2	onions, chopped
2 ¼ c.	¾ c.	chopped walnuts
12	4	cloves garlic
		paprika, salt, parsley—to taste

Rinse beans and **soak** overnight in fresh water. **Drain**. **Cook** the beans in enough water to cover and bring to a boil. Lower the temperature and **cook** until tender—about one hour. **Add** the chopped onions, the chopped walnuts, the garlic (pounded or crushed) and the seasonings. Let everything **boil** gently for about 5 minutes. **Turn off** heat and let it rest for 5 minutes.

(T) BEAN CASSEROLE

32	16	½ c. servings
4 c.	2 c.	each cooked or canned red beans limas and garbanzos or your choice
2	1	large onion, chopped
2	1	clove(s) garlic, minced
½ c.	¼ c.	date sugar
1 c.	½ c.	catsup, homemade
2 t.	1 t.	cumin
½ c.	¼ c.	red grape juice
6 T.	3 T.	lemon juice
		salt, to taste

Put beans into a 2 ½ quart casserole; **mix** lightly and set aside. In skillet **sauté** onions and garlic; **stir in** remaining ingredients. **Add** skillet mixture to beans in casserole; **mix** together. **Cover** and **bake** for about an hour at 325°. Or **simmer** the mixture in an electric slow cooker on medium for 1 hour.

(T) BLACK BEANS AND RICE

24	6	1 c. servings
4 c.	1 c.	black beans, soaked in cold water overnight, drained
12 c.	3 c.	water
4	1	medium onion, chopped fine
4	1	clove(s) garlic, minced
4	1	small green pepper, chopped
4 T.	1 T.	oregano
4	1	large tomato, chopped (opt.)
2 t.	½ t.	ground cumin
4 T.	1 T.	lemon juice
4 t.	1 t.	salt
4 c.	1 c.	long-grain rice, cooked fluffy and dry

Cook the soaked beans in the water for an hour, or until just tender. **Add** the rest of the ingredients except rice, **cover**, **cook** on low heat for another 20 to 30 minutes. **Add** the lemon juice just before serving. **Cook** the rice in slightly salted water until fluffy and dry. **Serve** the beans and rice in separate bowls, family style, or for a buffet.

Tossed green salad is delicious served over this with Salsa and Melty Cheese or an avocado dressing.

(T) BLACK-EYED PEAS WITH ONIONS

24	8	1 c. servings
18 c.	6 c.	water
3 c.	1 c.	black-eyed peas
3	1	large onion, chopped
1 ½ t.	½ t.	salt
	dash	garlic powder

Combine all ingredients in kettle. **Bring** to boil. **Simmer** until peas are tender—about 1 hour.

BREAD DRESSING CASSEROLE

24	½ c. servings
1 ½ lb.	loaf whole grain bread
2 c.	onions, chopped
2 c.	fresh parsley, minced
4 c.	green celery, chopped
2	large, unpeeled apples, grated
2 t.	salt
2 t.	sage
2 t.	marjoram
1 t.	thyme
2 c.	walnuts, chopped coarsely
1 c.	chicken style seasoning broth

Cut bread into small cubes. **Add** onions, parsley, celery, nuts and apples. **Combine** and **stir in** the four dry seasonings. **Add** chicken style seasoning to moisten. **Stir** gently. **Bake** in casserole at 350°.

(T) BULGHUR PILAF

24	4	½ c. servings
1 ½ c.	¼ c.	minced onion
6 c.	1 c.	bulghur wheat
12 c.	2 c.	vegetable broth (see Index)
1 ½ t.	¼ t.	oregano, crumbled
¾ t.	⅛ t.	thyme, crumbled
		salt, to taste

In a large skillet add 1-2 T. water. **Sauté** onion over medium heat for 2 minutes. **Add** bulghur wheat, and continue to sauté until golden. **Add** broth, oregano, thyme, and salt. Bring to a **boil**, reduce heat, **cover**, and **simmer** slowly for 20-25 minutes, or until tender and liquid is absorbed. **Serve** hot, garnished with freshly chopped parsley.

CARROT NUT LOAF

25	8	½ c. servings
Blend smooth:		
3 c.	1 c.	smooth soy milk or water
¾ c.	¼ c.	peanuts
Add:		
1 ½ c.	½ c.	oatmeal
6 c.	2 c.	carrots, grated
4 ½ c.	1 ½ c.	tomatoes chopped
3 c.	1 c.	dry whole wheat bread crumbs
¾ c.	¼ c.	chopped parsley
3 t.	1 t.	salt
3 t.	1 t.	green pepper, chopped

Combine and **bake** at 375° 45 minutes for loaf or 30 minutes for muffin tins.

CARROT RICE LOAF

24	6	1 c. servings
10 c.	2 ½ c.	carrots
2 c.	½ c.	roasted peanuts
3 c.	¾ c.	sesame milk (¾ c. water + ¼ c. sesame seeds)
4	1	small onion
2 t.	½ t.	salt
2 t.	½ t.	sage
6 c.	1 ½ c.	cooked brown rice
2 c.	½ c.	whole wheat bread crumbs

Blend milk, ground peanuts, carrots, onion, salt and sage in blender until smooth. **Add** to rice and bread crumbs and **mix** well. **Bake** in casserole 1-1 ½ hours (until firm in center) at 350°.

CHICK PEA A LA KING

10	servings

Soak 1 c. garbanzos in 3 c. water for several hours. **Add** 2 t. chicken style seasoning. **Cook** until tender. **Sauté** in water ½ c. green onion and ½ c. peeled eggplant.

Blend until smooth the following:

3 c.	water or garbanzo liquid
½ c.	cashew pieces
4 t.	sesame seeds
2 T.	chicken style seasoning
¼ c.	whole wheat flour or unbleached flour
½ t.	salt

Add onions and eggplant, then **add** 1 ½ c. frozen green peas and 2 large pimientos diced, and the garbanzos. **Cook** until thickened, **stirring** carefully to keep from scorching. **Serve** over cooked brown rice or whole wheat flat noodles. Bake 20-30 minutes at 350°.

(T) CHILI

24	12	1 c. servings
12 c.	6 c.	cooked kidney or pinto beans
12	6	small onions, chopped
6	3	cloves garlic, minced
4 c.	2 c.	tomato sauce
2 qt.	1 qt.	whole tomatoes, chopped
4 c.	2 c.	water, if beans are too dry
4 T.	2 T.	oregano
4 t.	2 t.	cumin or chili seasoning (see Index)
		salt, to taste
1	½	lemon juice
2 T.	1 T.	mild peppers

Place all in large pot and **simmer** for 30-40 minutes. **Serve** hot.

CORN PIZZA

24	6	½ c. servings
4 c.	1 c.	ground whole corn cooked in
12 c.	3 c.	water
4 t.	1 t.	salt,
12 c.	3 c.	cooked corn grits

Cook whole corn in water and salt. **Spread** on baking sheet ¼" to ⅛" thick. Next **layer** the sauce.

16 c.	4 c.	tomato sauce
4	1	can(s) sliced olives
4	1	small eggplant(s) or zucchini
8 t.	2 t.	basil
4 t.	1 t.	each, marjoram, oregano
		onion and garlic salt, to taste

Then **top** with Melty Cheese (see Index). **Bake** at 350° for 30-45 minutes or until baked and brown.

COUNTRY CROQUETTES

24	6	2 patty servings
4 c.	1 c.	soaked, drained soybeans
3 c.	¾ c.	water
2 t.	½ t.	Vege-Sal
4 T.	1 T.	chicken-style seasoning (see Index)

Blend the above ingredients and **add**:

2 c.	½ c.	millet ground fine or rice flour
4	1	medium grated potato
4	1	stalk(s) celery, chopped fine
4	1	onion(s), chopped fine

Mix well and **shape** into patties, using ¼ c. per patty. **Roll** in crumbs. **Bake** at 350° for 45 minutes to 1 hour.

CREPES WITH VEGETABLES

24	8	3 crepe servings
4 ½ c.	1 ½ c.	whole wheat flour (try pastry)
4 ½ c.	1 ½ c.	rolled oats
2 ¼ t.	¾ t.	salt
13 ½ c.	4 ½ c.	soy milk, or
12 c.	4 c.	water +
3 c.	1 c.	soy flour
¾ c.	¼ c.	thinly sliced green onions (or dried onion flakes)

Mix first three ingredients and **add** soy milk or water plus soy flour and onions. **Blend** very thoroughly. **Bake** on crepe iron.

Filling:

Stir fry until crispy tender:

3	1	clove garlic, minced
9	3 c.	shredded cabbage (regular or chinese)
6 c.	2 c.	carrots (2" long julienne strips)
18 oz.	6 oz.	frozen pea pods
15 oz.	5 oz.	can water chestnuts
1 ½ c.	½ c.	chopped green onion

Put the following in a bowl and **mix**.

1 c.	⅓ c.	soy sauce
6 t.	2 t.	cornstarch or arrowroot
6 T.	2 T.	apple juice concentrate

Add to vegetable mixture. **Cook** and **stir** to thicken. **Spoon** hot filling into warm crepes. May **serve** with gravy if desired.

(T) EGGPLANT

24	6	½ c. servings
4	1	eggplant (strips)

Cook in:

1 c	¼ c.	salt water with
4 c.	1 c.	celery, cut thin diagonally

When crispy done, **add**:

16 oz.	4 oz.	can pimiento, chopped
¾ c.	3 T.	chopped parsley
4	1	clove(s) garlic
2 t.	½ t.	oregano
½ t.	⅛ t.	dill
		salt to taste
½ c.	4 T.	lemon to taste

Mix. Heat thoroughly. **Serve** over hot rice.

EGGPLANT ENCHILADAS

24	8	1 tortilla servings
24	8	corn tortillas, wrapped and put in oven to heat at 325° for 15 minutes
6 c.	2 c.	tomato sauce
2 ¼ t.	¾ t.	each cumin, oregano and chili powder (see Index)

Stir well and set aside.
Sauté in:

1 ½ c.	½ c.	water
1 ½ c.	½ c.	chopped onion
6	2	cloves garlic, minced
4 ½ c.	1 ½ c.	tomatoes, diced
9 c.	3 c.	eggplant, peeled and diced
1 ½ c.	½ c.	ripe olives
9 T.	3 T.	chopped green peppers
1 ½ t.	½ t.	chili powder (see Index)

Remove from heat.

Put ½ c. of tomato sauce mixture into a baking dish, 8" x 10" or equivalent. **Add** 1 c. sauce to eggplant mix. **Put** about ½ c. eggplant mix in each tortilla, **roll** up and put seam side down in baking dish. **Spoon** remainder of sauce over center of enchiladas. **Bake** uncovered 350° for 20-30 minutes. **Serve** with hot Melty Cheese (see Index).

(T) FALAFELS (GARBANZO PATTIES)

24	12	3 falafel servings
2	1	medium onion, chopped fine
2 c.	1 c.	mashed potatoes
2	1	bunch parsley, minced
6 c.	3 c.	cooked, mashed garbanzo beans
1 t.	½ t.	salt
2 T.	1 T.	lemon juice
2 t.	1 t.	ground cumin
2 t.	1 t.	paprika
2	1	clove garlic

Sauté the onion in 1 T. water until transparent. **Mix** all the ingredients together and **shape** into patties, using 2 T. per patty. **Place** on prepared, nonstick baking sheet. **Bake** at 350° 15 minutes. **Turn** and **bake** 10 more minutes. **Serve** hot in Pita Bread with cucumber, tomato, lettuce, green onion, and green onion dressing.

GARBANZO BURGERS

24	6	½ c. servings

Blend:

2 c.	½ c.	soaked garbanzos
2 c.	½ c.	water

Add and **mix:**

4 c.	1 c.	oatmeal
4 c.	1 c.	finely chopped walnuts
4	1	medium onion, chopped fine
4 t.	1 t.	chicken-style seasoning (see Index)
4 t.	1 t.	salt
4 T.	1 T.	soy sauce or equivalent
2 t.	½ t.	sage
½ c.	2 T.	nutritional food yeast

Let stand ½ hour. **Make** into burgers ½ cup each. **Bake** at 350° until brown.

GARBANZO RICE PATTIES

24	6	½ c. servings
6 c.	1 ½ c.	soaked or sprouted garbanzos (overnight) in ¾ c. water to cover

Blend above and **add** following:

6 c.	1 ½ c.	cooked brown rice
1 ⅓ c.	⅓ c.	chopped brazil or other nuts
2 t.	½ t.	onion powder
2 t.	½ t.	salt
4 t.	1 t.	chicken-like seasoning (see Index)
½ t.	⅛ t.	garlic powder

Drop by large spoonfuls on non-stick skillet. **Bake** at 350°, covered for 10 minutes. **Turn** and **cook** 10 more minutes. Reduce heat and **cook** 10 more minutes. **Serve** plain or with Tofu Sour Cream (see Index) or gravy.

GARBANZO TOMATO LOAF

24	6	½ c. servings
4 c.	1 c.	soaked garbanzos
4 c.	1 c.	canned tomatoes
1 c.	¼ c.	Bronners Bullion or Savorex
2 c.	½ c.	bread crumbs
8 t.	2 t.	onion powder
½ t.	⅛ t.	garlic powder
2 c.	½ c.	peanut butter —(lightly roast and grind nuts) (add enough water to make a spread.)

Blend all ingredients in blender until smooth. **Place** in top of double boiler and **steam** about 2 hours, or until well set up. Delicious as an entree or in sandwiches.

(T) GREEN RICE WITH VEGETABLES

25	12	1 c. servings
4 c.	2 c.	chopped onions
3 c.	1 ½ c.	chopped green peppers
2	1	15 oz. can(s) tomato sauce
4 c.	2 c.	white grape juice
4	2	bay leaves
4 t.	2 t.	oregano
6 c.	3 c.	cooked rice
2 c.	1 c.	cooked green peas
½ c.	¼ c.	chopped parsley

In large skillet **sauté** onions and green peppers in water until tender. **Add** tomato sauce, grape juice, bay leaves, oregano, and 1 t. salt. **Cook** 20 minutes. **Remove** bay leaves. **Combine** rice, peas, and 2 T. parsley. **Heat. Toss** lightly. **Form** into a border on platter. **Place** hot cooked vegetables carrots, green beans, or zucchini down center of platter. **Spoon** sauce over vegetables and **sprinkle** with remaining parsley.

HAWAIIAN HAYSTACKS
with Oatmeal Noodles and Curry Sauce (opt.)

24	12	servings
12	6 c.	brown rice, cooked, dextrinized
4	2	recipes of Cashew Gravy (see Index) seasoned with
4 T.	2 T.	Savorex

The gravy is served over the rice with added fruits and nuts. The oatmeal noodles go on last for added crunch.

The following may be served in individual dishes, and are added by each person according to taste:

Tomatoes, diced; peppers, chopped; peanuts, chopped; macaroon coconut; diced green onion; crushed pineapple; chopped pimientos; chopped almonds, chopped bananas, raisins, diced cucumbers, grated or chopped radishes.

Instead of the gravy, some like a curry sauce. Recipe follows:

CURRY SAUCE
with coconut milk, for Hawaiian Haystacks

6 c.	3 c.	coconut milk
4 T.	2 T.	chicken-style seasoning
2 t.	1 t.	each coriander and cumin
1 t.	½ t.	bay leaf, powdered
1 t.	½ c.	green onions, chopped
½ t.	¼ t.	garlic powder
2 T.	1 T.	beef-style seasoning
6 T.	3 T.	arrowroot or corn starch

Sauté onion in 1 T. water. **Add** rest of ingredients. **Cook** to thicken. **Serve** hot over haystacks.

COCONUT MILK, for Curry Sauce

1 c.	unsweetened coconut
2 c.	boiling water

Let set for 15 minutes. **Blenderize. Strain.**

OATMEAL NOODLES
for Hawaiian Haystacks

1 T.	yeast
½ t.	salt
½ c.	hot water
1 ½ c.	rolled oats (add more if needed)
1 t.	dried onion flakes

Mix well. **Roll** thin. **Roll** up as for jelly roll and **slice** this like Ramen noodles. **Spread** to let rise 1 hour. **Bake** at 250° for 15 minutes. Increase to 350° and **bake** until crisp.

HAZELNUT TOFU BALL

48	24	2 T. balls
2 c.	1 c.	hazelnuts (filberts), slightly roasted
2 lb.	1 lb.	tofu
1 c.	½ c.	minced sweet onion or
½ c.	¼ c.	dried onion pieces
		salt to taste

Chop nuts in food processor. **Remove** ½ nuts, **add** tofu and onion and **mix** well. **Form** into 2 T. sized balls and **roll** in rest of nuts. **Wrap** in waxed paper or **put** in Tupperware to firm up. **Serve** with crackers.

(T) HERBED LENTIL LOAF

24	8	½ c. servings
5 ¼ c.	1 ¾ c.	lentils
12 c.	4 c.	water
	1	bay leaf
1 ½ T.	½ T.	each salt, soy sauce (or equiv.), garlic powder, celery seed, sage and thyme
1 ½ T.	½ T.	dried green pepper
6	2	medium onions, chopped
4 ½ c.	1 ½ c.	minced celery
6 c.	2 c.	rolled oats (oatmeal)
3	1	medium tomato(s), sliced

Wash lentils and bring to a **boil** with water, bay leaf, salt and seasonings. **Reduce** heat to simmer and **simmer** about 20 minutes. **Add** celery and onion. **Cook** for about 10 more minutes until lentils are tender and water is absorbed. **Preheat** oven to 350°. **Remove** lentils from heat, **remove** bay leaf and **stir** for a minute or so to **let cool** somewhat. **Add** oats and **mix** well. **Prepare** the bottom and sides of a 9" x 5" loaf pan, **line** the bottom with tomato slices and **sprinkle** with a little salt. **Press** lentil mixture into pan, then **bake** at 350° for about 40 minutes. Let **cool** a bit, then **separate** loaf from sides or pan with a spatula before **inverting** over a platter to serve.

Serving hints. To reheat slices Herbed Lentil Loaf, **pan-fry** or **pan-steam** them in a little stock, perhaps with a bit of soy sauce. To serve, **dribble** with hot melty cheese. Try cold slices in sandwiches with mayonnaise, lettuce, tomato, or pickle slices, etc. Herbed Lentil Loaf **freezes well**, too, in individual slices or larger pieces. **Serve** with Salad Bar.

(T) HERBED RICE

24	4	½ c. servings
4 ½ c.	¾ c.	onion
6 c.	1 c.	rice
12 c.	2 c.	water
3 t.	½ t.	each, marjoram, thyme, rosemary

Dextrinize rice. **Add** other ingredients and **bake** in 350° oven 1 hour or **cook** in kettle until done (1 hour).

HOLIDAY LOAF

30	10	½ c. servings (172 calories/serving)
3 c.	1 c.	water
¾ c.	¼ c.	garbanzos, soaked several hours or overnight

In dry blender **chop**:

1 ½ c.	½ c.	almonds
1 ½ c.	½ c.	sunflower seeds

Drain soaked garbanzos, **blenderize** with ½ c. water. **Combine** the above in mixing bowl with:

4 ½ c.	1 ½ c.	water
3	1	onion, chopped
1 ½ c.	½ c.	celery, chopped
3 c.	1 c.	oatmeal
3 c.	1 c.	seasoned dry crumbs
3 T.	1 T.	chicken-like seasoning
3 t.	1 t.	marjoram
3 t.	1 t.	salt

Press into prepared Pyrex loaf pan. **Bake** at 350° for 45-60 minutes.

LASAGNA WITH PINTO BEANS

24	8	1 c. servings
6 c.	2 c.	pinto beans, cooked
3 c.	1 c.	onion, chopped
3	1	medium carrot, chopped
3	1	clove garlic, minced
9 c.	3 c.	tomatoes, chopped with juice
3 t.	1 t.	each, salt, date sugar, oregano, basil and onion powder
6 c.	2 c.	tofu
¾ c.	¼ c.	crumbly cheese (see Index)
18-24	6-8	uncooked lasagna noodles, or to make two layers
3	1	recipe(s) melty cheese (see Index)

Combine all ingredients except the last 4. Bring to a **boil** and **simmer** 15-20 minutes. **Spoon** a thin layer of hot sauce in flat baking dish. **Place** uncooked lasagna noodles in flat baking dish. **Spoon** a layer of sauce and then layer of crumbled tofu. **Drizzle** with melty cheese. **Make** another layer sauce, noodles, sauce, tofu and melty cheese. Let **set** several hours to soften noodles—or overnight. **Bake** 45-60 minutes at 350° or until bubbly and lightly brown. If it sets a few minutes before serving, it will be easier to serve.

(T) LENTIL EGGPLANT CASSEROLE

24	8	1 c. servings
3	1	medium eggplant
6	2	medium onions, chopped
12	4	cloves garlic, minced
3 c.	1 c.	lentils soaked overnight in 4 c. water
1 ½ c.	½ c.	rice, rinsed
12	4	medium tomatoes, chopped
9 t.	3 t.	salt
3 T.	1 T.	curry seasoning (without) (see Index)

Bake at 350° 1 ½ hours or until rice and lentils are cooked.

LENTIL ROAST

24	6	1 c. servings
8 c.	2 c.	cooked lentils
4 c.	1 c.	cashew milk
4 c.	1 c.	fine bread crumbs
4 c.	1 c.	chopped walnuts
4 t.	1 t.	salt
2 t.	½ t.	sage
4 c.	1 c.	grated carrots
4 c.	1 c.	grated celery
4 T.	1 T.	food yeast

(handwritten: Check Dook I or just add ¼ cup (Cashew) to 1 cup Water Raw)

Combine, bake at 350° about 1 hour.

(T) LIMA BEAN CREOLE

24	8	½ c. servings
9 c.	3 c.	cooked lima beans
Add:		
3 T.	1 T.	green pepper, chopped
6 T.	2 T.	onion, grated
3 t.	1 t.	salt, if needed
Stir in:		
3 c.	1 c.	tomato juice
1 ½ c.	½ c.	tomato paste
3 T.	1 T.	flour

Place in casserole and **bake** in 350° oven for 30-45 minutes or until hot and bubbly.

MACARONI SHELLS

Partially **cook** shells. **Stuff** with mixture of tofu, celery, onion, chopped greens, seasonings. Make a thin white sauce or tomato sauce. **(Use** ½ c. red or white grape juice as part of the liquid.) **Pour** enough over to cover. Let stand a few hours or overnight. **Bake** at 250° for 1 hour, then 350° for 15 minutes.

MILLET BALLS

25	10	½ c. servings
1 ⅔ c.	⅔ c.	dry soy beans (2 c. soaked)
Grind or **blend** with onions		
⅔ c.	¼ c.	sunflower seeds—coarse ground
3 ¾ c.	1 ½ c.	cooked millet (½ c. cooked 1 hr. in 2 c. water with ½ t. salt)
⅔ c.	¼ c.	chopped brazil nuts
2 ½ c.	1 c.	dry bread crumbs (whole wheat)
1 ¼	½	large onion(s), ground or blended
⅝ t.	¼ t.	oregano
1 ¼ t.	½ t.	salt
1 ¼ c.	½ c.	fine dry bread crumbs or cereal crumbs
1 ¼ t.	½ t.	paprika

Combine all except last two ingredients. **Let stand** 5-10 minutes. **Form** into balls. **Roll** in crumbs and paprika. **Bake** at 350° for 40 minutes. **Serve** with gravy, tomato or tartar sauce.

MILLET BALLS GOURMET

20	10	½ c. servings

Soak ⅔ c. raw soybeans overnight in about 3 c. water. **Drain** soaked soybeans and **whiz** in blender:

4 c.	2 c.	soaked soybeans
1 c.	½ c.	water
2	1	medium onion
Combine above mixture with:		
3 c.	1 ½ c.	cooked millet*
1 c.	½ c.	slivered almonds
½ c.	¼ c.	sunflower seeds
2 c.	1 c.	seasoned bread crumbs (Pepperidge Farm or see recipe for Herb Seasoned Bread Crumbs)
1 t.	½ t.	salt

Let **stand** 5-10 minutes, **form** into balls. **Roll** in ½ c. seasoned crumbs. **Bake** on lightly greased cookie sheet or **line** pan with liner paper. **Bake** at 350° for 40 minutes. **Serve** with tomato sauce if desired.

***Cook** millet by **steaming** ½ c. millet in 2 c. water and ½ t. salt until soft, approximately 45 minutes.

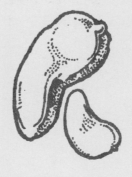

MILLET PATTIES

24	6	½ c. servings
6 c.	1 ½ c.	millet, cooked
4	1	medium onion, chopped fine
1 c.	4 T.	nutritional yeast, opt.
2 c.	½ c.	water
2 c.	½ c.	rolled oats
½ c.	2 T.	soy sauce or equivalent
2 c.	½ c.	sesame seeds, ground
4	1	clove(s) fresh garlic

Blend water, onion, garlic, and seeds in blender until chunky. **Pour** into mixing bowl and **add** remainder of ingredients. **Place** by spoonfuls (**flatten** to shape like patties) on prepared cookie sheet. **Brown** in oven at 375° for about 25-30 minutes.

MILLET PATTIES II

24	12	⅓ c. servings
8 c.	4 c.	cooked millet (To cook, use 4 c. water to 1 c. millet)
1 c.	½ c.	peanut butter
2 T.	1 T.	soy sauce or equivalent
4 T.	2 T.	onion powder
2 t.	1 t.	garlic salt
1 t.	½ t.	celery seed
½ t.	¼ t.	thyme
¼ t.	⅛ t.	cumin

Combine all ingredients well. **Form** into patties, place on prepared cookie sheet. **Bake** at 350° until nicely brown. **Turn** patties once. **Serve** with gravy.

MILLET PATTIES III

24	8	2 patty servings
3 c.	1 c.	almonds, ground very fine
12 c.	4 c.	millet, cooked with ½ t. salt
1 ½ t.	½ t.	garlic granules
1 ½ t.	½ t.	ground celery seed
1 ½ c.	½ c.	parsley, finely chopped

Form into ¼ cup patties. **Bake** at 375° until lightly brown, 30-40 minutes. **Serve** hot with gravy, salsa or savory sauce (see Index).

MILLET AND SQUASH PATTIES

24	8	patties
3 c.	1 c.	peeled and cooked winter squash
6 c.	2 c.	millet, rinsed
9 ¾ c.	3 ¼ c.	water
1 ½ t.	½ t.	celery salt
3/16 t.	1/16 t.	sage
1 ½ t.	½ t.	oregano

Bring to boil, covered. **Simmer** 40-50 minutes. **Let** cool and **add**:

18	6	green onions, minced
¾ c.	¼ c.	fresh, minced parsley or equivalent of dry
6 T.	2 T.	bread crumbs or more

Mix together until mixture will hold shape. **Add** more crumbs if mixture too wet. **Make** patties of ⅓ c. each. **Brown** both sides in oven. **Serve** with gravy.

NOODLE CASSEROLE

25	5	1 c. servings
10 c.	2 c.	cooked noodles (soy, wheat, etc.)
2 ½ c.	½ c.	almonds, slivered
2 ½ c.	½ c.	soy cheese
5 T.	1 T.	dried parsley flakes (or ¼ c. chopped fresh parsley)
5	1	pimiento, chopped
2 ½ t.	½ t.	onion powder
5/8 t.	⅛ t.	garlic powder
10 c.	2 c.	golden sauce (see Index)

Combine all ingredients. **Sprinkle** top with bread crumbs or food yeast flakes. **Bake** in casserole—about 30 minutes at 350°.

NOODLES

24	4	servings
36 oz.	6 oz.	noodles, cooked
12 T.	2 T.	each poppy, sesame and caraway seed or dill
3 c.	½ c.	chopped olives
1 ½ c.	¼ c.	chopped pimiento
3 t.	½ t.	salt
6 c.	1 c.	tofu, blended smooth

Heat thoroughly. **Serve** with Zucchini Special, hot rolls, green salad with Italian dressing. Lemon Pie for dessert.

NOODLES ORIENTAL STYLE
with Sauce

24	4	1 c. servings
3 lb.	8 oz.	whole wheat spaghetti or noodles
6 lb.	1 lb.	broccoli spears, thinly sliced
18	3	stalks celery, thinly sliced
24	4	onions, thinly sliced
1 ½ c.	4 T.	soy sauce or equivalent
¾ c.	2 T.	heaping, arrowroot flour

Slivered almonds or toasted sunflower seeds for garnish

Prepare noodles. While noodles are boiling, in a large skillet or wok **sauté** the broccoli with 2-3 T. water; when it changes color—to bright green, **add** celery, and **stir fry** a few minutes. **Drain** noodles reserving cooking liquid. **Dilute** arrowroot in water (use ½ c. cold water). Then **mix** with 2 c. of noodle water. **Pour** immediately over the vegetables, return to heat and **stir** until the sauce is thick. **Season** with soy sauce or similar flavor. **Pour** sauce over noodles and garnish with almonds.

You can use any combination of vegetables—chunks of fried tofu also are nice to use.

ONION DILL CASSEROLE

24	6	½ c. servings
8 c.	2 c.	diced onions
8	2	red peppers, diced
1 c.	¼ c.	chicken-like stock
4	1	clove garlic, minced
8 c.	2 c.	cooked brown rice
4 c.	1 c.	tofu
1 ⅓ c.	⅓ c.	minced fresh dill (or 1 T. dried)
1 ⅓ c.	⅓ c.	minced fresh parsley
1 ⅓ c.	⅓ c.	whole wheat bread crumbs
¾ c.	3 T.	nutritional food yeast flakes

Combine the onions, red peppers and stock in a large frying pan. **Cover** and **cook** over medium-low heat until vegetables are limp. **Add** garlic and **cook**, uncovered, until all liquid in the pan has evaporated. In a large bowl, **fold** together the onion mixture, rice, tofu, dill, parsley and 2 T. food yeast and **pour** into a 9" square baking dish. **Combine** the bread crumbs, 1 T. food yeast and 2 T. chicken-like stock in a small bowl, and **sprinkle** this mixture over the top of the casserole. **Bake** at 375° for 30 minutes.

(T) ONIONS AND RICE

Blanch onions in water. **Take out** center and **fill** with mixture of rice, parsley, chopped onion and a little nut milk. **Sprinkle** with seasoned bread crumbs and **dribble** with melty cheese. **Brown** lightly under broiler.

(T) PASTA CASSEROLE

24	4	1 c. servings
6	1	green pepper, chopped
6	1	red pepper, chopped
6 c.	1 c.	cubed yellow summer squash
6 c.	1 c.	cubed zucchini
12 c.	2 c.	cooked, hot pasta (corn, wheat)

Sauté chopped peppers. **Sauté** summer squash and zucchini in another pan. **Season** with chicken-like seasoning. **Layer** pasta, squash, peppers. **Serve** with hot melty cheese.

PASTA WITH VEGETABLES
with Tofu Sauce

24	6	1 c. servings
3 lb.	¾ lb.	whole wheat or spinach fettucini noodles
8-12 c.	2-3 c.	assorted fresh vegetables (cauliflower or broccoli florets, sliced carrot, zucchini, leeks, etc.)

Tofu Sauce:

4 lb.	1 lb.	tofu
1 c.	4 T.	sesame seeds, ground fine
½ c.	2 T.	food yeast
¾ c.	3 T.	fresh lemon juice
2 t.	½ t.	salt
4 t.	1 t.	grated lemon zest
2 t.	½ t.	garlic and onion powder

Cook the noodles. **Prepare** and **steam** vegetables until barely tender. While vegetables are steaming, **crumble** tofu into blender or food processor bowl and **add** sesame seeds, lemon juice and lemon zest. **Process** until completely smooth. **Place** cooked noodles on platter. **Add** hot vegetables and **dribble** over with tofu sauce. **Serve** at once. **Serve** extra sauce. Try sauce also on baked potato.

PECAN LOAF OR BALLS

24	8	3 patty servings
3 c.	1 c.	pecans
6 c.	2 c.	rice
12 c.	4 c.	bread crumbs, blended
4 ½ c.	1 ½ c.	water
¾ c.	¼ c.	sunflower seeds, ground
2 c.	⅔ c.	flour
3	1	medium onion, chopped
3 t.	1 t.	salt
3 t.	1 t.	basil

Make into loaf or ¼ cup balls. **Bake** 40 minutes at 350°.

PINE NUT RISSOLES

32	*16*	*½ c. servings*

Filling:

4 c.	2 c.	Walnut Bulghur (see Index)
4 c.	2 c.	cooked brown rice
2 c.	1 c.	pine nuts
2 t.	1 t.	dried parsley or equivalent fresh
½ t.	¼ t.	each sage and thyme

Mix with

2	1	recipe Cashew Gravy (see Index)

Make gravy as recipe, **adding:**

1 c.	½ c.	minced onions
2 T.	1 T.	Savorex

Crust:

1 ½ c.	¾ c.	cashew nuts
3 c.	1 ½ c.	hot water
1 t.	½ t.	salt
4 T.	2 T.	date sugar or 3 dates

Blend until smooth. **Add:**

2 T.	1 T.	yeast
6 c.	3 c.	whole grain flour

Mix dough, kneading lightly. **Roll** out dough. **Put** filling down the center and **fold** dough over, squeezing dough to make a seam. **Cut** in 1-2" slices and **place** seam *down* in prepared pan.

Bake at 350° or until golden brown. **Serve** with gravy. Same as used in the filling, or your choice.

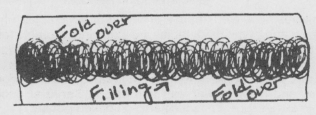

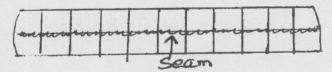

RICE WITH PEAS

32	*16*	*½ c. servings*
½ c.	¼ c.	chicken-style seasoning
¼ c.	2 T.	white grape juice
2 t.	1 t.	soy sauce or equivalent
3 c.	1 ½ c.	peas (frozen)
2 c.	1 c.	green onion, diced
12 c.	6 c.	cooked brown rice, hot

Mix gently. **Serve** hot.

RICE VERSATILE

(Cumin-Rice)

2 c.	brown rice, dextrinized
5 c.	water
1 t.	salt
2 T.	cumin

This is nice served with gravy or a tomato sauce.

Other seasonings: Omit the cumin. (1) Use tomatoes, onion, sweet basil, garlic. (2) Tomatoes and chili powder (see Index). (3) Celery, onion, tofu, soy sauce, pimiento.

Or if a dessert is needed:

(1) Shredded apples, dates or raisins
(2) Pineapple, cashew cream
(3) **Serve** plain with one of the fruit toppings.

(T) SAVORY MACARONI

24	*8*	*1 c. servings*
18 c.	6 c.	tomato juice
1 c.	⅓ c.	soy sauce or equivalent
3	1	clove garlic, minced
7 ½ c.	2 ½ c.	whole grain macaroni
3 ¾ c.	1 ¼ c.	canned tomatoes
1 ½ c.	½ c.	almonds
6 T.	2 T.	food yeast
3 t.	1 t.	onion salt
	pinch	sweet basil

Combine tomato juice, soy sauce and garlic in a 2 ½ quart saucepan. Bring to a boil. **Add** macaroni, **cook** until almost tender. **Whiz** remaining ingredients in blender until smooth. **Add** to macaroni. **Pour** into an oiled 12" x 8" baking dish. **Bake** at 450° until liquid is nearly all evaporated.

(T) SAVORY PATTIES

24	*4*	*⅓ c. patties*
7 ½ c.	1 ¼ c.	cooked soybeans (may use commercially canned)
12 T.	2 T.	chopped onions
2 t.	⅓ t.	salt
¾ c.	2 T.	tomato juice (omit if using baked beans with tomato sauce)
6 t.	1 t.	sage
6 T.	1 T.	seasoned salt

Grind beans through a food chopper or food processor. Lightly **brown** the onions in nonstick pan. **Combine** all ingredients and **mix** well. **Shape** into patties. **Roll** in crumbs (popcorn, ground is very good) and **bake** patties in oven—350° for 20 minutes.

SAVORY WAFFLES

24	4	waffles
18 c.	3 c.	water
12 c.	2 c.	rolled oats
3 c.	½ c.	each rolled wheat, rye and soy flour

Combine well in blender and **let set** about five minutes. Then **add:**

6 t.	1 t.	dried sweet red pepper
3 c.	½ c.	diced green pepper
3 c.	½ c.	minced onion
3 c.	½ c.	sliced olives
6 t.	1 t.	food yeast
1 ½ t.	¼ t.	minced garlic

Pour into hot waffle iron. **Be sure** batter is not too thick. It should be rather thin. **Bake** until no more steam escapes and lid lifts easily. These can be crisped in a toaster before serving.

Serve with: Seasoned Beans (see Index), lettuce, cucumbers, tomatoes, onion, salsa and guacamole.

SEVEN-GRAIN PATTIES

48	24	⅓ c. patties
5 c.	2 ½ c.	7-grain cereal
8 c.	4 c.	water
½ c.	¼ c.	soy sauce or equivalent
4 t.	2 t.	sage
2 t.	1 t.	onion powder
1 t.	½ t.	salt
1 c.	½ c.	each chopped nuts and sunflower seeds

Bring water and seasonings to **boil**. **Add** nuts, seeds and grains. **Cook** 30-45 minutes without stirring, or until grain is cooked. **Form** into patties—⅓ c. each, or your choice. **Bake** in 350° oven to brown. **Serve** in pita bread, on buns or with gravy.

SOY MILLET LOAF

24	12	½ c. servings

Blend smooth:

4 c.	2 c.	soaked soybeans
1 c.	½ c.	water
3 c.	1 ½ t.	celery seed, powdered
1 T.	½ T.	onion powder
2 t.	1 t.	vegetable salt
3 T.	1 ½ T.	soy sauce or equivalent

Pour into a bowl and **add:**

3 c.	1 ½ c.	cooked millet
½ c.	¼ c.	raw cashew nuts
2 T.	1 T.	peanut butter
½ c.	¼ c.	ground, raw sunflower seeds
6	3	slices whole grain bread, crumbled

Mix all. **Form** into patties or **spread** 1"-2" deep in prepared pan. **Bake** at 350° for 45 minutes to one hour.

SPAGHETTI PIE

24	6	1 c. servings
1 ½ lb.	6 oz.	spaghetti
4 c.	1 c.	tofu
2 c.	½ c.	chopped onion
1 c.	¼ c.	chopped green pepper
4	1	8 oz. can(s) tomatoes, cut up
4	1	6 oz. can(s) tomato paste
4 t.	1 t.	date sugar
4 t.	1 t.	dried oregano, crushed
2 t.	½ t.	garlic salt
2 c.	½ c.	Pimiento cheese or Melty cheese

Cook the spaghetti according to package directions; **drain** (should have about 3 c. spaghetti). **Blend** and add to spaghetti ¼ c. ground sesame seeds, ½ t. each garlic, onion, parsley, and chicken-like seasoning. **Form** spaghetti mixture into a "crust" in a prepared 10" pie plate. **Spread** mashed tofu over bottom of spaghetti crust.

In skillet **cook** ½ c. cubed eggplant, ½ c. cubed zucchini, onion, and green pepper until vegetables are tender. **Stir in** undrained tomatoes, tomato paste, date sugar, oregano, and garlic salt; **heat** through. **Turn** mixture into spaghetti crust. **Drizzle** with melty cheese. **Bake**, uncovered, in 350° oven for 20 minutes or until it browns slightly.

(T) SPAGHETTI
with Zucchini Sauce

24	6	1 c. servings

Main dish for a delicious, easy dinner. Serve with tomato and cucumber salad and a fresh fruit pie.

4 c.	1 c.	diced green pepper
4	1	medium onion, sliced
8	2	medium zucchini, sliced (about 6 cups)
12 c.	3 c.	diced tomatoes
2 t.	½ t.	salt
4	1	bay leaf
1 t.	¼ t.	basil leaves
1 t.	¼ t.	oregano leaves
32 oz.	8 oz.	corn or whole wheat spaghetti
		melty cheese

In large skillet or pot, **sauté** onion in hot water until crisp-tender. **Add** zucchini, tomatoes, salt, bay leaf, basil and oregano. **Simmer** covered for 15 minutes; **uncover** and **simmer** 10 minutes longer. **Discard** bay leaf. Meanwhile, **cook** spaghetti as directed on package; **drain**. **Serve** spaghetti topped with zucchini sauce and melty cheese.

SWEET AND SOUR TOFU

24	4	¼ c. servings

3 lbs.	½ lb.	tofu
1 ½ c.	¼ c.	rice, millet, or other cooked grain
1 ½ c.	¼ c.	water
3 t.	½ t.	garlic powder
6 T.	1 T.	soy sauce or equivalent

Drain tofu and **slice** into ½" cubes. **Blend** in the blender the grain, water, garlic powder and soy sauce. **Dip** the cubed tofu to coat into the blended grain mixture, then **roll** in bread crumbs. **Place** on a sprayed cookie sheet and **brown** in a 350° oven until crispy.

SWEET AND SOUR TOFU SAUCE

24	8	¼ c. servings

3 c.	1 c.	tomato sauce
3 c.	1 c.	unsweetened pineapple chunks in juice
¾ c.	¼ c.	crushed pineapple
6 T.	2 T.	lemon juice
1 ½ t.	½ t.	salt

Bring to **boil** and then **stir in** 1 T. cornstarch mixed with a little water. **Stir** and **cook** to thicken. **Place** crisped tofu on a warm platter and **pour** the sauce over the pieces. **Garnish** with parsley, or **serve** over brown rice. For special occasions you might add grapes cut in half. This is all compatible with a fruit meal.

TASTY TOFU TIMBALES

24	6	2 timbale servings

4 lb.	1 lb.	fresh tofu
2 ⅔ c.	⅔ c.	rolled oats
1 c.	¼ c.	food yeast flakes
1 c.	¼ c.	chopped pecans or other nuts
½ c.	2 T.	soy sauce or equivalent
4 t.	1 t.	onion powder
½-1 t.	⅛-¼ t.	garlic salt

Drain and **mash** tofu. **Combine** with all ingredients. **Knead** 2-3 minutes. **Form** into ¼ cup timbales. **Bake** at 425° for 30 minutes. **Serve** with gravy.

TOFU BURGERS

24	12	⅓ c. servings

1 c.	½ c.	bulghur
2 c.	1 c.	water
1 ½ t.	¾ t.	salt
1 lb.	½ lb.	firm tofu
1	½	medium onion, minced
1 T.	½ T.	each basil, oregano
½ t.	¼ t.	cumin
4 T.	2 T.	nutritional yeast
1 ½ c.	¾ c.	whole wheat flour or quick oatmeal

Bring water to a boil with ¼ t. salt, **add** bulghur and **simmer** for 5-10 minutes until water is absorbed. **Mash** tofu, **add** ½ t. salt, and seasonings, onion, nutritional yeast. **Mix**. **Mix** cooked bulghur with tofu mixture and **stir** until cool enough to handle. **Add** flour and **press** together into flat patties. May use ice cream **scoop**—**press** flat ½" to ¼". **Place** on prepared cookie sheet. **Bake** at 350° for 20-25 minutes.

TOFU BURGERS II

24	6	⅓ c. servings

4 lb.	1 lb.	tofu, well drained
2 c.	½ c.	loosely packed, shredded carrots
½ c.	2 T.	minced onion (green preferred)
¼ c.	1 T.	toasted sesame seeds, ground
1 t.	¼ t.	salt
8 t.	2 t.	soy sauce or equivalent

Mash tofu and **combine** all ingredients, **mix** well, **knead** 2 or 3 minutes. **Moisten** hands and **form** 6 (or 24) large burgers. **Cook** slowly on both sides until golden, either in nonstick baking dish in the oven or in a nonstick covered skillet on top of the stove. **Serve** in a bun with all the trimmings, or as an entree with vegetables.

TOFU CORN BALLS

24	12	2 ¼ c. servings
4 c.	2 c.	tofu
4 c.	2 c.	mashed potatoes
4 t.	2 t.	salt
2 t.	1 t.	paprika
4 c.	2 c.	cornmeal mush
2 c.	1 c.	bread crumbs
4 t.	2 t.	chicken-style seasoning
1 t.	½ t.	garlic salt

Make ball the size of walnuts. **Roll** in crumbs. **Bake** at 350° for 30 minutes or until heated and slightly brown.

TOFU HOT SANDWICH

24	6	½ bun servings
2 lb.	½ lb.	firm tofu
2	½	large onion, chopped
2	½	green pepper, chopped (opt.)
1 t.	¼ t.	garlic powder, or
8	2	cloves fresh garlic
1 t.	¼ t.	salt
2 t.	½ t.	each oregano, basil, or Italian-style herbs to taste
4 c.	1 c.	tomato sauce
12	3	muffins or buns, halved

Drain and **mash** tofu to crumbly consistency. **Put** in a pan on medium heat. **Add** onion, green pepper, and garlic and **sauté** for 2-3 minutes. **Add** salt and herbs and **stir** for a few more minutes until most of the moisture from the tofu has evaporated. **Add** tomato sauce, **mix**, and **simmer** on medium-low heat until vegies are tender, stirring occasionally. **Toast** buns or muffins and **cover** each half with tofu mix. If desired, top with melty cheese and **broil** until cheese is bubbly.

Chili Joes: Same directions, but **replace** the basil and oregano with 2 t. soy sauce or equivalent and ¾ t. cumin. **Add** 1 ½ c. cooked kidney or pinto beans along with the tomato sauce. This makes enough for 6-8 English muffins halves (3-4 muffins). **Broil** if desired.

TOFU NOODLES (macaroni)

25	5	1 c. servings
4 ½ lb.	14 oz.	noodles/macaroni, cooked
5	1	medium onion
5 c.	1 c.	walnut bulgher burger (see Index)
5 c.	1 c.	cashew gravy (see Index)
5 c.	1 c.	tofu blended with ½-1 t. lemon juice, or 1 c. mayonnaise (see Index)
5 T.	1 T.	chicken-like seasoning (see Index)
1 ¼ t.	¼ t.	each sweet basil, oregano, rosemary and season salt (see Index)

Sauté onion in 1 T. water. **Mix** well all ingredients and seasonings. **Bake** in 350° oven for 45 minutes. Could used 1 c. bulghur with more seasonings instead of walnut wheat burger.

TOFU SQUARES

24	6	2 slice servings
4	1	brick(s) regular tofu
Broth:		
2 c.	½ c.	tofu water or plain water
2 t.	½ t.	cumin
½ c.	2 T.	chicken-like seasoning

Slice each brick of tofu into 12 slices. **Place** in broth made of tofu water, cumin and chicken-like seasoning. Let set for at least one and a half hours. **Drain** well. **Place** on large cookie sheet that has been sprayed with vegetable spray. **Broil** under broiler until edges turn crisp. **Serve** hot with gravy. Use broth for some of gravy liquid.

TOFU STROGANOFF

24	4	1 c. servings
3	½	medium onion, diced
6 c.	1 c.	diced celery
4 lb.	10 oz.	tofu, cut in ½" cubes
1 c.	3 T.	soy sauce or equivalent
4 ½ c.	¾ c.	water
3 t.	½ t.	salt (to taste)
1 ½ c.	¼ c.	red grape juice
¾ c.	2 T.	whole wheat pastry flour
4 ½ lb.	¾ lb.	fettucini noodles
4 ½ c.	¾ c.	tofu mayonnaise

Heat water to cook pasta in a large pot. In 1 T. water **sauté** onion until soft. **Add** tofu cubes and **sauté** 5 minutes. **Add** soy sauce and water. **Simmer** 1 minute, then **add** seasonings and grape juice. **Simmer** 1 minute more, then **add** flour carefully, while stirring, to thicken mixture. **Reduce** heat. **Serve** over pasta.

TOFU STROGANOFF II

24	12	½ c. servings
2 lb.	1 lb.	tofu
1 c.	½ c.	soy sauce, or
¼ c.	2 T.	Savita in ½ c. water
2 t.	1 t.	garlic powder
1 t.	½ t.	cumin
2	1	medium onion, minced
8 c.	4 c.	eggplant, peeled, quartered, sliced
1 t.	½ t.	salt (to taste)
1 t.	½ t.	basil
2 T.	1 T.	green pepper, chopped fine
½ c.	¼ c.	white grape juice
2 c.	1 c.	tofu—seasoned with lemon and salt

Cut tofu into pieces about ¼" x ½" x 1", then **marinate** as follows: **place** in a jar or small deep bowl, **add** soy sauce or savita mixture, garlic, cumin, and green pepper plus just enough water to cover. Let tofu marinate for at least 20 minutes. **Sauté** in fry pan with the tofu, onion and eggplant for 4-5 minutes and **stir** gently. **Add** salt, if needed and basil. **Reduce** heat to low. **Cook**, covered for 10 minutes, **stirring** occasionally and adding a bit of marinade or water as needed to keep from burning. **Add** grape juice and blended tofu. **Heat** through but don't allow to simmer. **Add** a little soy sauce or extra herbs at this point if needed to correct the seasoning. **Serve** on top of flat whole wheat noodles: spinach or plain. Also delicious on brown rice or whole wheat bread or toast.

TOFU VEGIE BAKE

24	6	1 c. servings
½ c.	2 T.	soy sauce or equivalent
½ t.	⅛ t.	garlic powder
3 lb.	¾ lb.	firm tofu
1 t.	¼ t.	salt
4 t.	1 t.	rosemary
2 t.	½ t.	each sage, thyme
6	1 ½	medium onions, sliced thinly
6	1 ½	medium tomatoes, sliced thinly
12 c.	3 c.	total zucchini, summer squash eggplant and/or green pepper, sliced thinly
4 c.	1 c.	melty cheese

Preheat oven to 350°. **Mix** soy sauce and garlic powder with ½ c. water to make marinade for tofu. **Slice** tofu in slices about ½" thick, and **pour** marinade over. **Marinate** for at least 10 minutes. **Mix** salt and herbs together in a small bowl or glass. In an 8" x 8" or larger covered casserole, **layer** ingredients in it as follows: Onions, drained tofu, tomato, vegies, melty cheese, sprinkling some of the salt-herb mixture on each layer. **Pour** tofu marinade evenly over all, **cover**, and **bake** at 350° for about 45 minutes until vegies are tender.

TOMATO QUICHE

24	4	¼ pie servings
6	1	partially baked 8" pie crust (Almond-Sesame) (see Index)
3 c.	½ c.	each, onion, pepper, chopped
6	1	clove garlic, minced
24	4	red ripe medium tomatoes
3 t.	½ t.	each, salt, oregano, basil
1 c.	3 T.	each, tomato paste, chopped parsley
12 c.	2 c.	cashew gravy (see Index) (use 3 T. cornstarch)
72	12	pitted olives, preferably green ripe

Sauté onions, green pepper, garlic in 1 T. water. **Add** chopped tomatoes, herbs and salt. **Combine** with gravy and **pour** into crust. **Top** with olives. **Bake** until firm and lightly brown in 350° oven for 30-45 minutes. **Serve** with green salad (lettuce, sprouts, cucumber, frozen peas—any or all) and whole grain hot rolls.

(T) VEGETABLE BURRITOS

24	8	burritos

Sauté in small amount of water:

12	4	6" long zucchinis, sliced
12	4	medium carrots, diced
3	1	chopped onion
3	1	bell pepper, chopped
3 c.	1 c.	eggplant
¾ t.	¼ t.	each oregano, garlic salt, cumin, basil

Stir fry above. **Quarter** 4 small tomatoes and put in to warm. **Serve** in warm flour tortillas, with melty cheese sauce. May **add** chopped olives. Eat with a fork. **Serve** with a salsa (optional).

VEGETABLE SAUCE
for Spaghetti or Lasagna

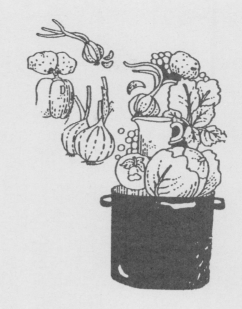

24	12	½ c. servings
2 lb.	1 lb.	beets
4 lb.	2 lb.	butternut or butter cup squash—washed, cubed
6	3	onions, diced
4	2	green peppers, diced
		oregano, basil, bay leaves, mild pepper, etc., to taste
		soy sauce or equivalent, to taste

Scrub beets. **Boil** in water until easily pierced with a fork. **Sauté** in water: onions, and squash until braised, then **add** green peppers, and **sauté** a few more minutes. **Puree** cooked beets in a blender with cooking liquid. **Add** to sautéed vegetables and **season** with herbs to taste. **Simmer** sauce for 30 minutes. **Add** soy sauce or equivalent. **Cook** a few more minutes and **serve** with noodles.

For lasagna, **brush** a casserole with lecithin and **line** with a layer of uncooked noodles, then **cover** with a layer of sauce. **Make** sauce a little thinner and be sure it is very hot. **Crumble** over tofu. Tofu mashed with a little tahini or sesame butter will yield a rich tasting cheese substitute. Continue with noodle layers and sauce and tofu and then **bake** in a moderate 350° oven for about 40 minutes—or until bubbly.

WALNUT BULGHUR
(use as burger)

12 c.	4 c.	
3 c.	1 c.	walnuts
13 ½ c.	4 ½ c.	water
1 ½ c.	½ c.	onion flakes, dried
4 ½ t.	1 ½ t.	onion powder
¾ t.	¼ t.	garlic powder
6 c.	2 c.	bulghur wheat or cracked wheat

Blend walnuts and water until smooth. **Place** in sauce pan and **add** remaining ingredients. **Simmer** covered for 20 minutes. **Dry** out on cookie sheet at 150° all night or at 200° for 4-6 hours. Use as burger.

Mix together and **heat** 2 c. seasoned tomato juice and 4 c. dried mixture. **Heat** until juice is absorbed but not dried out. Delicious with added sautéed onions and green peppers. For use in tacos, spaghetti, enchiladas, pita bread, chili, tostados, etc.

Gravies and Sauces

AVOCADO TOPPING
for Baked Potatoes

30	15	2 T. servings
8	4 large	avocados, diced
1 c.	½ c.	sunflower seeds
½ c.	¼ c.	nutritional yeast
1 lb.	8 oz.	tofu, mashed
2	1	medium onion, chopped fine
1 c.	½ c.	celery, chopped fine
1 c.	½ c.	peppers, chopped fine
4	2	cloves garlic
1 t.	½ t.	Vegesal
2 t.	1 t.	lemon juice
2 T.	1 T.	parsley, chopped

Stir to thoroughly but gently mix.

CASHEW GRAVY

30	6	½ c. servings
Boil:		
10 c.	2 c.	water
2 ½ t.	½ t.	salt
Blend:		
5 c.	1 c.	water
2 ½ c.	½ c.	cashews
7 ½ T.	1 ½ T.	whole wheat flour
7 ½ T.	1 ½ T.	unbleached or golden white

Add above to boiling water, while stirring. **Cook** until thick. **Add** seasonings: 4 t. (1 t.) onion powder, 2 T. (2 t.) chicken style seasoning, and 4 t. (1 t.) yeast flakes.

COUNTRY GRAVY

24	6	¼ c. servings
8 c.	2 c.	hot water
2 c.	½ c.	cashew nuts
8 t.	2 t.	onion powder
8 T.	2 T.	cornstarch or arrowroot starch
2 t.	½ t.	salt

Blenderize smooth. **Cook** to thicken. Use as white sauce or **add** 2 T. Savita or Vegex and 1 T. nutritional yeast seasonings for gravy.

(T) GOLDEN SAUCE

24	8	¼ c. servings

This sauce is an excellent topping for cooked vegetables. In blender **combine:**

2 ¼ c.	¾ c.	hot water from vegetables
2 ¼ c.	¾ c.	cooked potatoes
2 ¼ c.	¾ c.	cooked carrots
3 T.	1 T.	lemon juice
1 ½	½ t.	salt

Blend until smooth. Serve hot.

(T) GRAVY I

24	6	½ c. servings
2 ⅔ c.	⅔ c.	whole wheat pastry flour, brown lightly
4 t.	1 t.	chicken-like seasoning
4 t.	1 t.	onion salt
8 T.	2 T.	food yeast flakes
12 c.	3 c.	water as needed
4 T.	1 T.	lemon juice
4	1	medium tomato, peeled, diced (Add lemon and tomato just before serving)

See directions for Gravy II.

(T) GRAVY II

24	8	¼ c. servings
1 c. + 2 T.	6 T.	whole wheat pastry flour
6 c.	2 c.	water
1 ½ t.	½ t.	garlic powder
1 ½ t.	½ t.	onion powder
⅜ t.	⅛ t.	celery seed
3 t.	1 t.	Vegex
1 ½ c.	½ c.	sautéed onions, chopped fine

Be sure to **dextrinize,** or brown flour in pan. It can be done in a dry skillet on low to medium heat until lightly brown. Do not burn. **Take off** the heat and **cool** then **add** cold water. **Stir** with gravy maker utensil until smooth. Then put on heat and **add** rest of ingredients. Bring to boil and **stir** constantly. **Cook** until thickened nicely. **Serve** on baked potatoes, entree, loaf, or casserole that requires gravy.

(T) GRAVY III

24	8	1/3 c. servings
6	2	potato, pureed
6 c.	2 c.	water
1/2 c.	2 2/3 T.	chopped onion
1 1/2 t.	1/2 t.	food yeast
3 t.	1 t.	Vegex
3/4 t.	1/4 t.	garlic powder
3/4 t.	1/4 t.	onion powder

Mix together and **cook** until potato and onion are done and gravy is a clear, thick mixture.

(T) GRAVY for Oatburgers

24	8	1/2 c. servings
3	1	onion, sliced
3 t.	1 t.	salt
1 1/2 t.	1/2 t.	basil
3 c.	1 c.	water or vegetable stock
1 1/2 c.	1/2 c.	oatmeal flour
9 c.	3 c.	boiling water

Blenderize vegetable stock with flour. **Add** to boiling water with other ingredients. **Stir** often. **Cook** 20-30 minutes.

MELTY CHEESE

2 quarts	3 cups	
12 oz.	4 oz.	jar pimientos
6 T.	2 T.	arrowroot or cornstarch
1 1/2 c.	1/2 c.	cashew nuts
3 c.	1 c.	water
6 t.	2 t.	salt
3/4 c.	1/4 c.	food yeast
3/4 c.	1/4 c.	oat flour (finely ground oatmeal)
6 T.	2 T.	lemon juice
3 t.	1 t.	onion powder

Blenderize well.

4 1/2 c.	1 1/2 c.	boiling water

Add to boiling water and **cook** until thick.

(T) PINEAPPLE CHILI SALSA

2 quarts	2 cups	
2 c.	1/2 c.	very ripe pineapple chopped
2 c.	1/2 c.	mango or papaya chopped
2 c.	1/2 c.	sweet red pepper chopped
2 c.	1/2 c.	yellow pepper
1 c.	1/4 c.	jicama chopped
4	1	clove garlic
4 t.	1 t.	chili powder (see Index)
8 t.	2 t.	fresh coriander, chopped fine
8 t.	2 t.	fresh basil, chopped fine
8 t.	2 t.	fresh mint, chopped fine
8 T.	2 T.	lemon juice
4 t.	1 t.	soy sauce
4	1	juice of 1 lime

Make chunky in food processor. **Marinate** 2 hours before serving.

SAVORY SAUCE

24	8	1/4 c. servings
6 c.	2 c.	water
9 T.	3 T.	raw cashews
1 1/2 t.	1/2 t.	veg. salt
1 c.	1/3 c.	ground sesame seeds
9 T.	3 T.	arrowroot powder
3 t.	1 t.	onion powder, or
3	1	large onion
3 T.	1 T.	whole wheat flour
6 T.	2 T.	Bronners Bullion or soy sauce or equivalent

Put above ingredients in blender and **blend** well. Then **pour** into a kettle and **cook** over low heat until thick. **Serve** over cooked rice, potatoes, or toast.

For a delicious spread for bread or toast, **mix** sauce half and half with ground cashews or other nuts. Can be frozen.

SESAME SAUCE

Makes 1/4 c.

For green beans, spinach, broccoli, or carrots.

	1 T.	toasted sesame seeds, ground
	1 T.	white grape juice
	1 T.	soy sauce
	1 T.	lemon juice

Stir well and **serve**.

SESAME TOPPING

Gently dry roast in fry pan 1 cup of sesame seeds until they are lightly browned. **Add** 1 t. salt and then **grind** briefly in the Moulinex or blender. Topping for salads, baked potatoes, etc.

TAHINI SAUCE

3 c.	1 c.	sesame seeds
1 ½ c.	½ c.	water
1 ½ t.	½ t.	salt
3 T.	1 T.	lemon juice

Blend smooth. **Serve** on vegetables.

TART & PEPPY SAUCE

Makes ½ c. +

For new potatoes, boiled, sliced fresh tomatoes, or use as a vegetable dip.

½ c.	Mayonnaise (see Index)
3. T.	Cashew Milk if Mayonnaise is too thick
½ c.	water cress leaves (no stems)

Blend until creamy and smooth.

TOFU SOUR CREAM

2 cups

¼ c.	cashews (optional)
¼ c.	water or fruit juice for toppings for fruit dishes
1 lb.	tofu
1 t.	salt
1 ½ t.	lemon juice

Blend until smooth. **Serve** on fruit pies, fruit crisps, etc.

TOFU TOPPING

Tofu (blended smooth). **Add** onion, salt, dill, fresh lemon to taste, and garlic powder. **Serve** on potatoes or broiled tomatoes cut in half crosswise.

(T) TOMATO SAUCE

3	*quarts*
2-28 oz.	cans whole tomatoes, or
4	pints canned tomatoes
4	cloves garlic, or
½ t.	garlic powder
1 c.	carrots, cut up
2 c.	celery with leaves cut up
2 c.	fresh onions cut up, or
1 c.	dried onion flakes
½ t.	salt (to taste)

Drain the liquid from the tomatoes, **put** in blender. **Add** garlic, carrot, and **whiz** at high speed until liquefied. **Add** celery and **chop** until fine. Using fresh onion, add onion and **chop**. **Pour** into large sauce pan. In blender, **chop** tomatoes a few seconds at low speed and **pour** into large sauce pan. If using dried onion flakes, **stir in**. Bring to boil, **cover** and **simmer** one hour. **Add** salt to taste. May be frozen.

CREAMY DRESSING

64	16	2 T. servings
4 c.	1 c.	water
4 c.	1 c.	cashews
½ t.	⅛ t.	garlic salt
2 t.	½ t.	onion salt
1 c.	¼ c.	dry onion
½ c.	2 T.	lemon juice
¼ c.	1 T.	yeast flakes
2 c.	½ c.	tomatoes or tomato sauce

Whiz in blender. Use as dressing, sandwich spread or sauce for vegetables.

(T) FRENCH DRESSING

32	16	2 T. servings
4 c.	2 c.	tomato or V-8 juice
½ c.	¼ c.	lemon juice
4 T.	2 T.	dry onion flakes and parsley
4 T.	2 T.	dry green pepper flakes
Pinch		each, marjoram, thyme, savory, sage, oregano, basil

Blend. Let stand several hours.

(T) FRENCH SALAD DRESSING

5 c.	2 ½ c.	
2 c.	1 c.	lemon juice
2 c.	1 c.	water
1	½	cucumber
1	½	onion
½	¼	bell pepper
½ t.	¼ t.	garlic powder
½ t.	¼ t.	salt
1 t.	½ t.	celery seed
1 t.	½ t.	dill weed
2 T.	1 T.	parsley

Blend and **chill** overnight.

GREEN DRESSING

4 c.	1 ½ c.	
4 c.	1 c.	cashew base or soy mayonnaise
4	1	avocado
1 t.	¼ t.	salt
4 T.	1 T.	fresh lemon juice
1 c.	¼ c.	onion, green
1 c.	¼ c.	celery tops

Make cashew base blending cashews in water or use soy mayonnaise. **Blend** all ingredients together.

(T) HERB DRESSING

24	8	2 T. servings
3 c.	1 c.	water, bring to boil
4 ½ T.	1 ½ T.	arrowroot or cornstarch (mixed with 2 T. water—add to boiling water)

Cook above to thicken.
Add:

3 t.	1 t.	onion powder
1 ½ t.	½ t.	each, dill and garlic
5 T.	5 t.	lime juice or lemon
3	1	cloves garlic, minced
6 T.	2 T.	fresh basil, or
1 T.	1 t.	dry basil
2 T.	2 t.	parsley, fine
2 T.	2 t.	chives or green onions, chopped
1 ½	½	each, red & green pepper, chopped
⅜ t.	⅛ t.	salt

Mix and **chill** before serving.

ITALIAN DRESSING

24	8	2 T. servings
3 t.	1 t.	salt
¾ c.	¼ c.	lemon juice
1 ½ c,	½ c.	grape juice, white
3 T.	1 T.	finely chopped green onion
3 T.	1 T.	finely chopped parsley
3 T.	1 T.	finely chopped dill pickle
3	1	clove(s) garlic
3 T.	1 T.	finely chopped pimiento (add last)

Put all in jar. **Shake** vigorously to blend. **Refrigerate** several hours; **remove** garlic clove before serving. Makes about 1 cup. Use with green salads.

(T) LEMON HERB SALAD DRESSING

Squeeze fresh lemon juice over a salad. **Season** with your preference of herbs and seasoning powders such as: garlic powder, onion powder, Italian seasoning.

MAYONNAISE
uncooked and simple

Almonds
Distilled water
Lemons
Seasonings, (paprika, Dr. Bronner's Balanced Mineral Seasoning, Nature's Gourmet herbal seasoning, and/or Bernard Jensen's Organic Seasoning and Instant Gravy, etc.)

Place almonds in blender, along with some water, and **liquefy** on high speed until well blended, **adding** more water as needed, but keeping the mixture as thick as possible. When almonds are well blended, **add** seasonings to taste and **blend** again. **Juice** lemon(s); **add** lemon juice to taste; and **blend** once more. This will thicken the mixture. **Serve** with fresh vegetables or fruits as a salad dressing, as an ingredient in other salad dressings, or as a vegetable dip or sandwich spread base.

NO OIL MAYONNAISE

1	quart	
1 ½ c.	boiling water	
3 T.	arrowroot or cornstarch—mixed with	
½ c.	water	

Add to boiling water and bring to boil again.
Remove from heat.
Blend in blender:

1 c.	water
½ c.	oatmeal
1 c.	cashews

Add starch mixture while still hot.
Add:

½ c.	fresh lemon juice-or less
1 T.	salt
2 t.	garlic powder

Blend well and **refrigerate.**

PEANUT DRESSING

16	8	2 T. servings
1 ½ c.	¾ c.	pineapple juice
4 T	2 T.	peanut butter
4 T.	2 T.	lemon juice
1 t.	½ t.	salt
½ t.	¼ t.	paprika

Blenderize well. **Serve** on any carrot salad or fruit salad.

RICE MAYONNAISE
SWEET AND SOUR

16	8	2 T. servings
4 T.	2 T.	cashews
4 c.	2 c.	well cooked rice
½ c.	4 T.	pineapple juice concentrate
½ t.	¼ t.	each salt, onion powder, celery salt
1 c.	½ c.	boiling water
2 t.	1 t.	lemon juice or to taste

Blenderize until smooth. **Chill** and **serve.**

SALAD DRESSING

24	12	2 T. servings
2 c.	1 c.	water
1 c.	½ c.	cashew nuts
4 T.	2 T.	fresh lemon juice
2 t.	½ t.	salt
2	1	clove garlic
3-4 t.	1-2 t.	favorite seasonings
½ c.	¼ c.	red bell pepper or pimiento
4-8 T.	2-4 T.	pectin

Blend smooth. **Chill.**

(T) SIMPLE SALAD DRESSING

24	8	1 T. servings
1 ½ c.	½ c.	tomato juice
6 T.	2 T.	lemon juice
3 t.	1 t.	onion powder
3 t.	1 t.	dried parsley OR
3 T.	1 T.	fresh parsley
3 t.	1 t.	food yeast
	sprinkle	garlic powder

Mix. Blend or **shake** well. **Serve** on green salad.

SOY MAYONNAISE

32	16	2 T. servings
2 c.	1 c.	soybean base (see Index)
2 c.	1 c.	garbanzos with 1 c. liquid
⅔ c.	⅓ c.	raw cashews
⅔ c.	⅓ c.	sesame seeds
3 t.	1 ½ t.	salt
2 T.	1 T.	lemon juice
2 cloves	1 clove	garlic
1 t.	½ t.	celery seed
½ t.	¼ t.	onion powder

Blend. If too thick, **add** water.

SUNFLOWER SEED DRESSING

4 c.	2 c.	
2 c.	1 c.	sunflower seeds
3 c.	1 ½ c.	water

Blend until thoroughly smooth.
Add:

2 t.	1 t.	salt
2 t.	1 t.	chicken style seasoning (see Index)
½ t.	¼ t.	garlic granules
2 t.	1 t.	onion powder
½ t.	¼ t.	each dill, red sweet pepper
⅔ c.	⅓ c.	fresh lemon juice

Blend until very smooth. **Add** more sunflower seeds if not thick enough, and **adjust** lemon juice if you like more. Chill for a few hours.

TARTAR SAUCE

32	16	1 T. servings
2 c.	1 c.	tofu mayonnaise
2 T.	1 T.	each chopped onion, green pepper, parsley
1 t.	½ t.	paprika to taste
1 t.	½ t.	dill weed

THOUSAND ISLAND DRESSING

1	¼ c.	
1 c.		mayonnaise (see Index)
1 T.		mild taco sauce
1 T.		chopped green pepper
1 t.		chopped pimiento
1 t.		chopped chives

Blend ingredients thoroughly. **Chill. Serve** on lettuce wedges.

TOFU MAYONNAISE *also see Pg 78 at bottom*

28	2 T. servings
3 c.	tofu
½ c.	fresh lemon juice, scant
¼ c.	water
½ t.	onion powder
⅛ t.	marjoram
⅛ t.	savory
⅛ t.	rosemary
1 t.	dill weed
¼ t.	sweet basil
½ t.	salt - or to taste

Put all ingredients in blender and **blend** until smooth. Then **add** to salad and **mix** well. Try: ½ t. each: basil and onion and ¼ t. garlic. Try: Tofu blended with the onion, garlic, and salt. **Fold in** avocado cubes and chopped pimiento.

(T) TOMATO SALAD DRESSING

24	8	2 T. servings
3 c.	1 c.	tomato sauce
6 T.	2 T.	fresh tomato juice
3 t.	1 t.	dried onion
3 t.	1 t.	dried parsley
¾ t.	¼ t.	salt
⅜ t.	⅛ t	garlic powder

Combine all ingredients in jar with lid and **shake** well before using. **Add** tomato juice, if needed, to make the desired consistency.

Dressings, <u>Spreads</u>, Jams & BUTTER

AVOCADO SPROUT SANDWICH SPREAD

24	8	2 T. servings
2 ¼ c.	¾ c.	tofu
3	1	medium avocado
3 T.	1 T.	lemon juice
4 t.	1-2 t.	onion powder
1 ½ t.	½ t.	salt

Blend. Put on bread and **garnish** with alfalfa sprouts and parsley sprigs or **blend** some dried parsley in with avocado.

(T) BEAN SANDWICH SPREAD

24	4	¼ c. servings
6 c.	1 c.	cooked beans, drained quite dry
¾ c.	2 T.	onions minced finely
¾ c.	2 T.	celery minced finely
¾ c.	2 T.	fresh lemon juice or to taste
		salt/garlic salt to taste
9 T.	1-2 T.	no-oil soy mayonnaise

Mash beans and **add** other ingredients. **Add** lettuce leaf if desired.

CASHEW JACK CHEESE

24	12	2 T. servings
1 c.	½ c.	water
1 ½ c.	¾ c.	boiling water
¼ c.	⅛ c.	yeast flakes
2 t.	1 t.	onion powder
2 T.	1 T.	lemon juice
7 ½ T.	3 ¾ T.	Emes unflavored gelatin
1 ½ c.	¾ c.	raw cashews
1 T.	½ T.	salt
½ t.	¼ t.	garlic powder
3 T.	1 ½ T.	raw carrot

Put cold water and gelatin to soak for a few minutes in blender. **Add** boiling water and **blend**. **Add** all other ingredients and **blend** until smooth.

CHEESE

32	16	2 T. servings
4 c.	2 c.	water
¼ c.	⅛ c.	fresh lemon juice
⅔ c.	⅓ c.	flour
⅔ c.	⅓ c.	yeast flakes
¼ t.	⅛ t.	garlic powder
2 t.	1 t.	onion powder
6 T.	3 T.	arrowroot or cornstarch
4 oz.	2 oz.	pimiento
1 t.	½ t.	salt

Blend well. **Cook** to thicken, stirring.

CORN <u>BUTTER</u>

24	12	2 T. serving
2 c.	1 c.	cooked corn, drained
1 c.	½ c.	cooked millet
½ c.	¼ c.	finely ground coconut
½-1 t.	¼-½ t.	salt

Put all in blender and **blend** until very smooth.

CORN <u>BUTTER</u> II

60	20	2 T. servings
6 t.	2 t.	Emes unflavored gelatin
¾ c.	¼ c.	cold water
3 c.	1 c.	boiling water
3 c.	1 c.	well-cooked fine cornmeal
¾ c.	¼ c.	cashews
6 t.	2 t.	lemon juice (fresh)
1 medium	1-1 ½"	raw carrot

Put the cold water and gelatin in blender to soak for a few minutes. **Add** 1 c. boiling water and **blend**. **Add** all ingredients and continue blending until completely liquefied. **Pour** into serving container and **cool**.

<u>MILLET BUTTER</u>

1 cup Hot Cooked Millet   1 cup Water
1/3 Cup Coconut   3/4 – 1 teaspoon Salt
1/4 Cup Cooked Carrots (Optional)

BLEND until very smooth.
CHILL before using. Then use and
keep in fridge.
Carrots are used for colour and Vitamin A.

CORN BUTTER III

20	10	1/4 c. servings

Stir together:

| 1 c. | 1/2 c. | cold water |
| 6 T. | 3 T. | Emes gelatin |

Add to:

| 2 c. | 1 c. | boiling water |

Bring again to **boil**.

Put the hot mixture in blender along with:

2 c.	1 c.	hot cooked fine cornmeal
2/3 c.	1/3 c.	cashew nuts
6 T.	3 T.	medium raw carrot
1 1/2 t.	3/4 t.	salt
4 T.	2 T.	lemon juice (fresh)

Blend until very smooth. Adjust seasonings. **Pour** into serving dishes. **Cover** and **cool**. The mixture will be thick when cold.

"CREAMY CHEESE" FILLING

20	10	1/4 c. servings

2 lbs.	1 lb.	tofu
1 c.	1/2 c.	mayonnaise
2 T.	1 T.	lemon juice
4 T.	2 T.	chopped parsley
2 T.	1 T.	chicken-like seasoning (see Index)
		salt to taste

Blend tofu and mayonnaise until very smooth. **Add** other ingredients and **mix** thoroughly. Use thinly sliced variety bread to make sandwiches.

DILL CUCUMBER DIP OR SPREAD

4 c.	2 c.	

2	1	package tofu
2	1	medium cucumber peeled and cut in chunks
4 T.	2 T.	dill
4	2	medium cloves garlic
6 T.	3 T.	onion
		salt to taste

Blend well and **serve** as dip for raw vegetables, chips, or crackers.

EGGPLANT SPREAD

Peel eggplant. **Cook** in small amount of water. **Blend** with chopped green onion, garlic, lemon juice, dill weed and chopped fresh or dried parsley.

GARBANZO PEANUT DIP

24	6	1/2 c. servings

4 c.	1 c.	cooked garbanzos (very soft)
1 c.	1/4 c.	sesame seeds (grind first)
1 c.	1/4 c.	peanuts
2 t.	1/2 t.	salt
2 c.	1/2 c.	water
6 T.	1 1/2 T.	fresh lemon juice
1 1/3 t.	1/3 t.	garlic powder

Blend well in blender. **Adjust** seasonings to taste.

GARBANZO SESAME SPREAD

20	10	1/4 c. servings

4 c.	2 c.	garbanzos (canned)
1 c.	1/2 c.	whole sesame seeds
2 t.	1 t.	garlic
2 T.	1 T.	parsley flakes
6 T.	3 T.	lemon juice

Blend with enough water to make a thick spread.

HERB SPREAD

24	4	1/4 c. servings

3 lbs.	1/2 lb.	soft tofu
2-4 T.	1-2 t.	Savorex
1 1/2 t.	1/4 t.	garlic powder
3/4 c.	2 T.	chopped parsley

Thoroughly **mix** all ingredients. Use as a spread on toast rounds or crackers. Variation: **Spread** on French bread or rolls and **broil** for garlic toast.

HOMMUS TAHINI SPREAD

24	12	1/4 c. servings

4 c.	2 c.	garbanzos, drained
6	3	medium garlic cloves, chopped fine
1 c.	1/2 c.	garbanzo juice
2 t.	1 t.	salt
1/2 c.	1/4 c.	lemon (fresh)
2 c.	1 c.	tahini (sesame seeds ground fine)

Blend all—should be thin enough to spread.

(T) KIDNEY BEAN AND GARBANZO BEAN SPREAD

24	8	¼ c. servings
3 c.	1 c.	kidney beans
2 ¼ c.	¾ c.	garbanzo beans

Mash above with a fork or food processor.

1 c.	⅓ c.	chopped celery
1 c.	⅓ c.	chopped onion
3 T.	1 T.	lemon juice
1 t.	⅓ t.	salt

Add dill to taste. **Mix** together.

LENTIL DIP

24	12	¼ c. servings
6 c.	3 c.	lentils, well cooked
4	2	cloves garlic, minced
1 ½ t.	¾ t.	salt
½ t.	¼ t.	cumin
¼ t.	⅛ t.	chili powder (see Index)
½ c.	¼ c.	lemon juice
2 t.	1 t.	coriander leaves (cilantro)
4 T.	2 T.	tomatoes, finely chopped. Add last.

Cook lentils in water. **Combine** with other ingredients and **puree. Add** tomatoes.

NUT SPREAD

Add sesame and sunflower seeds (ground) to peanut butter.

OLIVE NUT FILLING

24	4	¼ c. servings
3 c.	½ c.	olives, chopped
1 ½ c.	¼ c.	nuts, chopped
¾-1 c.	2-3 T.	no-oil soy mayonnaise
12	2 stalks	celery, chopped finely

Mix ingredients. Use only enough mayonnaise to moisten.

OLIVE SPREAD

24	12	¼ c. servings
2	1	can pitted green ripe olives, sliced
4 c.	2 c.	rice-well cooked, without salt
¼ c.	2 T.	pimiento
¼ c.	2 T.	diced onion pieces or diced fresh
¼ c.	2 T.	lemon juice to taste

Blend cooked rice with juice from olives to spread consistency. **Mix** together. **Serve** generously on whole wheat toast with a slice of mild onion and tomato. **Serve** cold or broiled in oven.

PEANUT BUTTER DATE SPREAD

Slowly **add** ½ c. water to ½ c. peanut butter and **mix** well. **Add** ½ c. chopped dates and mash **well** with a fork (or use a blender). **Add** one or more of the following: 2 T. coconut, 1 T. lemon juice, or 2 t. sesame salt.

PIMIENTO SPREAD

20	10	¼ c. servings
4 c.	2 c.	garbanzos
¼ c.	⅛ c.	pimiento
½ c.	¼ c.	chopped celery
1 T	½ T.	parsley flakes
¼ t.	⅛ t.	onion powder
¼ t.	⅛ t.	salt

Blend.

PIZZA CASHEW CHEESE

24	12	¼ c. servings
1 c.	½ c.	water
⅔ c.	⅓ c.	Emes unflavored gelatin
4 c.	2 c.	hot, well-cooked fine cornmeal
1 c.	½ c.	cashew nuts
½ c.	¼ c.	lemon juice, fresh
2 T.	1 T.	onion powder
6 T.	3 T.	food yeast flakes
3 t.	1 ½ t.	salt
½ t.	¼ t.	garlic powder

Soak Emes in blender with ½ c. water. **Add** hot cornmeal and **blend** thoroughly. **Add** all other ingredients and continue blending until smooth. **Pour** into square container and **chill** until firm. This will be firm enough to slice or grate.

POCKET BREAD FILLING

48		*pita bread halves*
3 lb.		tofu, frozen, thawed and water squeezed out.

Crumble onto cookie sheet and **season** with onion, garlic, food yeast, chicken-like seasoning, paprika, cumin. **Bake** at 400° stirring often until slightly brown.

2		heads lettuce
1		pkg. frozen peas
1		can water chestnuts, chopped
½ c.		green onions, chopped
1 c.		pickles chopped
3		tomatoes, chopped

Mix gently with mayonnaise. **Fill** pita bread. **Stand** up in pan. **Place** in oven a few minutes to crisp up pita bread.

RICE AND CARROT <u>BUTTER</u>

32	16	*2 T. servings*
2 c.	1 c.	rice, hot, cooked
2 c.	1 c.	sliced carrots (raw)
½ c.	¼ c.	coconut
2 t.	1 t.	salt
		water

Blend thoroughly in blender, adding as much water as is necessary to blend mixture. **Add** salt to taste.

SANDWICH CHEESE

70	35	*2 T. servings*
2 c.	1 c.	water
⅔ c.	⅓ c.	rounded, Emes unflavored gelatin
2 ½ c.	1 ¼ c.	boiling water
6 T.	3 T.	food yeast flakes
3 t.	1 ½ t.	salt
3 c.	1 ½ c.	cashews
4 t.	2 t.	onion powder
½ t.	¼ t.	garlic powder
½ c.	¼ c.	fresh lemon juice
8 oz.	4 oz. jar	pimiento

Soak gelatin in water in the blender. **Pour** boiling water in blender and **blend**. **Add** all other ingredients and **blend** until smooth. Best if allowed to firm 18 to 24 hours.

SAVORY SPREAD

24	12	*2 T. servings*
¼ c.	⅛ c.	soy sauce or equivalent
¼ c.	⅛ c.	water
¼ t.	⅛ t.	garlic powder
1 c.	½ c.	sunflower seeds

Blend above ingredients.
Add:

1 lb.	½ lb.	tofu
1 c.	½ c.	green onion tops
¼ c.	⅛ c.	parsley

Blend.

SESAME SPREAD

Mix 1 T. lemon juice with ½ cup ground sesame seeds, then slowly **add** ¼ cup water and **mix** well until smooth. **Add** 1 T. savita (or more to taste), plus 2 T. finely chopped parsley, chives, watercress, or scallions, and **mix** again. Sesame spread is equally delicious in sandwiches with lettuce, cucumber, etc., or as a spread for crackers.

SPROUT SANDWICH FILLING

¼ c.	parsley chopped fine
2 c.	alfalfa sprouts
6 oz.	tofu
1 t.	any herbs
1 t.	caraway seeds
	fresh lemon juice

Mix the tofu and herbs. **Chop** the parsley and sprouts and **mix** with the other ingredients into the tofu. **Serve** in warm pita bread or toasted whole grain bread with a slice of tomato.

TOFU ALMOND SPREAD

	10	2 T. servings
Sauté:	¼ c.	ground raw almonds
	1 small	minced onion
	2 T.	soy sauce
Add:	1 pkg.	tofu, mashed
	⅛ t.	salt
	½ t.	onion powder
	dash	garlic powder

Blenderize well. **Chill** and enjoy on bread, crackers, zwieback or stuffing for celery sticks.

Alternate Method:

In food processor, put all ingredients:

½ c.	¼ c.	slightly roasted almonds
2 T.	1 T.	dried onion flakes
4 T.	2 T.	soy sauce
2 pkgs.	1 pkg.	tofu - 10.5 oz.
¼ t.	⅛ t.	salt
1 t.	½ t.	onion powder
⅛ t.	dash	garlic

Blend until smooth.

TOFU AVOCADO DIP

Take equal parts of mashed avocado and tofu and **thin** with water. **Season** to taste with salt and lemon juice. May also **add** garlic and onion powder—cumin if desired.

TOFU AVOCADO SPREAD

Makes 2 cups

1	carton tofu, mashed fine or blended

Put into bowl and **Add**:

1	avocado, diced
1	4 oz. jar pimientos, chopped
½ t.	salt

Adjust following to taste:

	salt
½ t.	onion powder
¼ t.	garlic, granulated
1 t.	fresh lemon piece

Stir gently.

TOFU DIP

32	16	2 T. servings
1 t.	½ t.	salt
2 lbs.	1 lb.	tofu
2 T.	1 T.	fresh lemon juice

Toast dried onion flakes in oven until browned. **Blend** into tofu along with seasonings of choice (dill weed, garlic powder, cumin, chili (recipe in Index)—use one or several.

TOFU PEANUT BUTTER BANANA SPREAD

28	14	¼ c. servings
24 oz.	12 oz.	tofu
1 c.	½ c.	peanut butter
3 c.	1 ½ c.	bananas
4 t.	2 t.	lemon juice
3 t.	1-2 t.	date sugar or apple juice concentrate

Combine and **serve** on whole wheat toast. **Top** with nuts or raisins.

TOFU SANDWICH SPREAD

20	10	2 T. servings
2 c.	8 oz.	soft tofu
1 c.	½ c.	celery, finely chopped
4	2	green onions with tops, sliced fine
		few sprigs parsley chopped
2 t.	1 t.	fresh lemon juice
½ t.	¼ t.	dill weed
½ t.	¼ t.	garlic powder
1 t.	½ t.	chicken style seasoning
1 t.	½ t.	celery salt
2 T.	1 T.	finely chopped pickles
½ t.	¼ t.	salt - or to taste
2	1	can(s) green, ripe olives, sliced

Mash tofu. **Add** and **stir** well other ingredients except the sliced olives which are for garnish. **Serve** on whole grain crackers, or toast.

TOMATO DIP

16	8	2 T. servings
2 c.	1 c.	tomatoes
2	1	green onion
¼ t.	⅛ t.	salt
2 T.	1 T.	roasted sesame seeds, ground
2	1	clove(s) garlic, minced

Whiz in blender until smooth.

(T) YEASTY SPREAD

24	8	2 T. servings
3 c.	1 c.	tomato juice, or V8 juice or another vegetable juice
6 T.	2 T.	soy sauce
¾ t.	¼ t.	powdered celery seed
¾ t.	¼ t.	powdered onion enough yeast flakes to thicken

Bring the first four ingredients to a rolling **boil**. **Allow** to cool and then **mix** with enough yeast flakes to give a good spread consistency. Use on crackers, toast or bread.

Dressings, Spreads, <u>Jams</u>

Jams and Jellies can be made with fresh fruits, canned fruits, or dried fruits, or a mixture of any or all.

Fruit juice, frozen, concentrate. **READ LABELS.** Many of these are not pure; they may have added aspartame or sugar even though they say "100% Natural." **Read** the fine print. Some of the more readily found pure juices are: apple, cherry, orange, pineapple, grape, and some mixtures of berry.

Juices may be thickened with Emes gelatin, arrowroot starch, tapioca or cornstarch—bring juice to **boil**, **add** thickener mixed with water and bring back to **boil**. Tapioca should be cooked until clear. Dried fruits—**soak** in juice or water over night or 2-4 hours. **Blend**. **Add** fresh fruit if desired.

When adding frozen fruit, it may be added when juice is still hot. It will cool the jelly or jam.

Some suggestions:

Grape juice—Add blueberries or boysenberries or marion berries.

Raspberry-Apple—Add raspberries or strawberries.

Cherry—Add cherries cut in pieces.

Orange-pineapple—Add pineapple or apricots.

Apricot juice—Add apricots.

APRICOT JAM

3	cups
1 c.	pineapple juice
2	tangelos or small oranges
2 c.	dried apricots

Soak apricots in juice over night or 2-4 hours. **Blend** all to the consistency you wish. If too thick, **add** water or juice, depending on desired sweetness.

BLUEBERRY JAM

1	can pure frozen grape juice concentrate
1	can water

Bring to **boil**. **Thicken** with:

4 T.	arrowroot or cornstarch

Add:

3	boxes frozen blueberries

This cools the jam and it can be served at once.

STRAWBERRY JAM

96 T.	48 T.	
		May use other fresh fruit.
4 c.	2 c.	fresh or frozen berries
8-10	4-5	rings dried pineapple

Pineapple or orange juice as needed for right consistency

Soak dried pineapple in juice. **Blend**. **Add** fresh fruit. **Blend**.

Vegetables

IDEAS WITH VEGETABLES

Carrot sticks, cauliflowerettes, tiny whole cooked beets (canned)—serve with dip.

Asparagus. **Remove** seals, **snap** off tough end. **Cut** into long, thin diagonal slices about 1 ½" long, ¼" thick. Have water boiling. **Put** asparagus in strainer and a few minutes before serving **cook** for 2 minutes, in boiling water, **drain** and **serve** with a dash of garlic salt.

Beets may be baked as potatoes in 325° oven for about 1 hour. **Peel** while hot.

Add sliced, cooked carrots to creamed celery.

Grate raw carrots, **add** to cole slaw, toss salads, or potato salad.

French Style Green Beans and Water Chestnuts may be put in casserole. **Cover** with Cashew Gravy. **Bake** 20 minutes. **Top** with slivered almonds and continue baking until bubbly.

(T) CARROT PATTIES

24	8	2 patty servings
3 c.	1 c.	soaked garbanzos (½ c. dry 1 c. water)
1 ½ c.	½ c.	water
1 ½ c.	½ c.	salt
6 t.	2 t.	chicken-like seasoning
6 c.	2 c.	shredded carrots

Place all ingredients except the shredded carrots in the blender. **Blend** until smooth. **Add** to shredded carrots, then **form** into ⅓ c. patties and **fry** at 250° in skillet or in medium hot nonstick frying pan until brown.

(T) CARROTS A LA ZUCCHINI

24	6	½ c. servings
2 c.	½ c.	water
12	3	medium carrots
16	4	zucchini squash
2 t.	½ t.	salt

Scrub the carrots and **slice** them. **Add** to the boiling water and **cook** ten minutes. **Scrub** the zucchini and **slice** them. **Add** zucchini and salt to the carrots and **cook** an additional 3-4 minutes until the vegetables are crispy-tender.

CORN AND LIMA BEANS

24	12	scant ½ c. servings
1 c.	½ c.	onion, chopped
4 c.	2 c.	lima beans
½ c.	¼ c.	water
5 c.	2 ½ c.	corn

Cook above ingredients until barely done. **Mix** milk and flour. **Add** to beans and corn. **Cook** a minute or two, then **add** tofu mayonnaise.

1 c.	½ c.	nut or soy milk
4 T.	2 T.	whole grain flour
½ c.	¼ c.	Tofu Mayonnaise
½ t.	¼ t.	salt or to taste

Paprika to **decorate—serve** hot.

CORN ON COB

Serve with Sesame Butter and soy sauce or equivalent. Corn is usually very tasty just plain. This might be an idea for less delicious corn.

(T) CREAMED ASPARAGUS

24	6	⅓ c. servings
48 oz.	12 oz.	asparagus
2 c.	½ c.	fine carrot
2 c.	½ c.	water
2 t.	½ t.	salt
1 c.	¼ c.	unbleached flour, dextrinized
10 c.	2 ½ c.	water
1 t.	¼ t.	basil
4 t.	1 t.	salt
½ t.	⅛ t.	garlic
4	1	pimiento, diced to decorate top

Cook first 4 ingredients 15-20 minutes. **Make** a gravy of remaining ingredients except pimiento. **Combine** all and **serve** over toast or in crepes.

CREAMED CORN

24	6	½ c. servings
4	1	medium onion(s) chopped
2 c.	½ c.	chopped grated pepper
8 c.	2 c.	corn
4 T.	1 T.	wheat flour
2 c.	½ c.	Soy or nut milk
		salt to taste

Cook onions and grated pepper and corn until crispy done. **Add** rest of ingredients. **Mix** well and bring to **boil** for 2 minutes. **Serve.**

CURRIED CORN

24	6	½ c. servings
4	1	onion, chopped
4	1	clove garlic chopped
2 c.	½ c.	diced green and red pepper
2 t.	½ t.	coriander
2 t.	½ t.	cumin
10 c.	2 ½ c.	corn
1 c.	¼ c.	water
2 t.	½ t.	salt
½ c.	2 T.	parsley, chopped
4 T.	1 T.	lemon juice

Cook all about 5-7 minutes. **Add** lemon juice and parsley.

(T) EGGPLANT DELIGHT

24	8	servings
4	1	eggplant

Wash and **peel** eggplant, **cut** into ¼" slices.

2 c.	½ c.	whole wheat flour
2 c.	½ c.	barley or oat flour
		enough water for creamy consistency

Dip slices into batter and then into finely ground whole wheat bread crumbs. **Place** on a prepared baking sheet. **Spread** with a tomato sauce made as follows:

32 oz.	8 oz.	tomato puree
1 t.	¼ t.	celery seed, ground
1 t.	¼ t.	garlic powder
4 t.	1 t.	Italian herb blend

May also use Hunts Tomato Sauce Special with the above herbs. **Top** with sliced olives. **Bake** 25-30 minutes at 375° or until tender.

(T) EGGPLANT SUPER

24	8	½ c. servings
3	1	medium eggplant, peeled, and finely chopped
3 c.	1 c.	chopped onion
9	3	fresh tomatoes chopped
		Salt, to taste
3 t.	1 t.	dried crumbled basil
9 T.	3 T.	(heaping) tofu mayonnaise in 1 t. wat

Sauté eggplant and onion until tender, **turning** frequently with pancake turner. When soft **add** tomatoes, salt, and basil. When the tomatoes are hot through but not cooked **add** the last ingredients. **Stir** through and **serve** at once.

GREEN TOMATOES

Sprinkle with salt and seasoning as you sauté both sides in oven or nonstick griddle.

GREENS AND BASIL

24	4	½ c. servings
24	4	large shallots (or onions) minced
1 ½ c.	¼ c.	chicken-like stock
6 lb.	1 lb.	beet greens
1 c.	3 T.	minced fresh basil OR
6 t.	1 t.	dried basil
6 T.	1 T.	toasted sesame seeds, ground

In a large frying pan over low heat, **cook** the shallots in stock until they are soft. (If using dried basil, **add** to pan with shallots.) **Wash** the beet greens well and **remove** the thick stems. **Shred** or leave them whole, **add** to the pan along with the basil, and **cook**, using only the water left clinging to the greens; **cook** only until they wilt. **Stir** over medium heat for a minute to evaporate any remaining liquid. **Sprinkle** with ground sesame seeds.

HERBED GREEN BEANS WITH SEEDS

	1	small onion, chopped
	2 T.	water
	½ t.	each basil, marjoram, chervil
	1 T.	fresh parsley or
	2 T.	chives or
	1 T.	dried chives
	⅛ t.	savory or thyme
	1	clove garlic minced or
	⅛ t.	garlic salt
	½ c.	sunflower seeds, slightly dry toasted
	½ t.	salt (or less)

Sauté small onion in water. Then **add** the herbs. **Cook** fresh green beans ½ to 1 cup per serving. Season with the above herbs.

HOT POTATO AND BROCCOLI SALAD

24	8	1 c. servings
18	6	potatoes, peeled & cubed
1 ½ c.	½ c.	water

Cook for 5 minutes, then **add:**

3 lb	1 lb	broccoli, peeled, cut in small pieces.

Cook 5 minutes, then **add:**

3	1	clove(s) garlic
1 ½ c.	½ c.	sliced celery
1 ½ c.	½ c.	slivered red onion.

Cook 5 minutes, then **add:**

2 ¼ t.	¾ t.	salt
¾ c.	¼ c.	lemon juice

Serve hot.

IDEAL POTATOES

24	8	1 c. servings
27	9	medium potatoes
6 c.	2 c.	cashew milk
3 T.	1 T.	food yeast
1 ½ t.	½ t.	onion powder
⅜ t.	⅛ t.	garlic

Boil potatoes with skins on. **Peel** and **shred**—medium or coarse—into shallow baking dish—a couple inches deep. **Heat** rest of ingredients—don't boil—just **heat**. **Salt** potatoes and **add** milk to them. **Bake** at 350° for 45 minutes.

ONION RINGS CRISPY

1	recipe Cashew Gravy, seasoned and cooked

Thin to a dipping consistency. **Cut** onion rings and dip in gravy. **Blend** toasted bread crumbs very fine. **Place** in plastic sack. **Put** the onion rings in the sack and **shake** to cover well. **Place** on cookie sheet. May stack 2 or 3 deep alternating. **Crisp** and **brown** in oven. **Serve** hot.

PARSNIP BALLS

2 c.	cooked mashed parsnips
½ c.	ground almonds
1 t.	salt
½ c.	chopped celery
1 c.	chopped onions
1 c.	dry bread crumbs (use ½ in recipe)

Combine and **make** into balls. **Roll** in crumbs - ½ cup. **Bake** at 375° for 30-45 minutes.

PARSNIP GARBANZO PATTIES

1	large parsnip, raw, med. shredded
½ c.	soaked garbanzos
¼ c.	water
½ t.	salt

Blend raw garbanzos in water, fine. **Combine** all. **Drop** by tablespoonfuls onto prepared cookie sheet. **Bake** at 375° until brown, 30-45 minutes.

PASTA WITH VEGETABLE SAUCE

24	8	½ c. servings

Cook pasta as per instructions.
Sauce:

1 ½ c.	½ c.	each, grated carrot, celery, onion zucchini, pepper
¾ c.	¼ c.	parsley
18 oz.	6 oz.	tomato paste
10 ½ c.	3 ½ c.	canned tomatoes or fresh
3 c.	1 c.	red grape juice
3 T.	1 T.	oregano
4 ½ T.	1 ½ T.	sweet basil

Cook to blend flavors. **Serve** hot. **Garnish** with parsley.

POTATO DUMPLINGS

24	6	servings
24	6	potatoes, ground fine
4	1	onion
4 c.	1 c.	oatmeal flour, ground
2 t.	½ t.	salt
4 t.	1 t.	onion powder
2 c.	½ c.	bulghur wheat

Make into balls. **Put** ½ t. seasoned tofu or pimientos in center. **Boil** gently for 30-45 minutes in a seasoned broth. Use the broth thickened to serve over potato dumplings.

POTATO NESTS

24	8	½ c. servings
12	4 c.	mashed potatoes, seasoned

Put potatoes in decorating bag and **squeeze** donut shape on baking dish. **Bake** until top is slightly brown. May **fill** with peas and carrots, baked or scrambled tofu, or other vegetables.

RED POTATOES
with Red Sweet Pepper Sauce

6	red potatoes, boiled in small amount of water (1 cup)
1	garlic, sliced thin
½ t.	salt
1 t.	crushed red pepper flakes
1 c.	sweet green pepper strips

Add the garlic, salt, red pepper and green pepper. **Cook** a few minutes. **Add** chives and serve.

ROASTED POTATOES with Vegetables

24	8	servings
18	6	potatoes, peeled and cut in eighths, lengthwise
6	2	large red peppers, cut in lengths
6	2	large green peppers, cut in lengths
24	8	small onions, quartered
24	8	cloves of garlic
6 t.	2 t.	dried rosemary, crumbled over the vegetables
3 t.	1 t.	salt
1 ½ c.	½ c.	water.

Cover and **bake** in oven until potatoes are done, about 45 minutes.

SPAGHETTI SQUASH

Have you ever tried spaghetti squash? It's available in the farmer's markets and in some stores in the fall. It's very low in calories and takes the place of noodles in a spaghetti dish. It can be cooked to perfection in the microwave (cut in half) and shredded with a fork into "noodles."

SPANISH EGGPLANT

32	8	½ c. servings
4 c.	1 c.	diced eggplant
½ c.	⅛ c.	diced, sautéed green pepper and onion
4 c.	1 c.	tomatoes cut
6 oz.	1 ½ oz.	tomato paste
1 t.	¼ t.	each, basil, salt, paprika
½ t.	⅛ t.	each, oregano, cumin
1 t.	¼ t.	garlic
4	1	bay leaf

Cook 20-30 minutes. Good as sauce for green beans, summer squash, etc.

SPINACH CASSEROLE

24	8	1 c. servings
15 slices	5 slices	whole wheat bread cubed
3 cans	8 oz.	water chestnuts
12 c.	4 c.	chopped spinach or
6-10 oz.	2-10 oz.	frozen chopped spinach
6 T.	2 T.	onion flakes
4 ½ c.	1 ½ c.	boiling water
2 ¼ c.	¾ c.	cashew pieces
¾ c.	¼ c.	yeast flakes
6 T.	2 T.	whole wheat flour
6 T.	2 T.	lemon juice
3 t.	1 t.	salt
1 ½ t.	½ t.	onion powder
12 oz.	4 oz.	pimiento or tomato
1 ½ t.	½ t.	parsley
27	9	bite size Shredded Wheat

Layer first three ingredients in 2 quart flat baking dish starting with bread cubes and ending with spinach on top. **Blend** the rest of ingredients except Shredded Wheat and **cook** until thick. **Pour** over layers. **Crush** Shredded Wheat and add to top. **Bake** at 350° 40 minutes.

STUFFED PEPPERS

24	4	1 cup servings
24	4	medium peppers (cook 5 minutes and drain)
12 c.	2 c.	corn
6 c.	1 c.	beans
3 c.	½ c.	Melty Cheese
		cumin
9 c.	1 ½ c.	tofu cubes

Fill with corn, beans, tofu and cheese. **Sprinkle** peppers with cumin. **Place** in baking dish. **Bake** 20 minutes or until well heated—375°.

(T) SUMMER SQUASH AND CARROT

24	8	½ c. servings
4 ½ c.	1 ½ c.	carrots, peeled and thinly sliced
4 ½ c.	1 ½ c.	yellow summer squash, cubed
3	1	medium onion, slivered
3	1	medium green pepper, diced
3	1	medium red pepper, diced or
¾ c.	¼ c.	pimiento strips
1 ½ t.	½ t.	salt

Begin **stir frying** carrots in 1-2 T. water 5-8 minutes. **Add** other ingredients and fry until barely tender. **Serve** at once. **Add** small amount of water to keep from burning. Colorful.

SUNSHINE CARROTS

24	4	½ cup servings
30	5	medium carrots, sliced crosswise on bias (1" pieces)
6 T.	1 T.	orange juice concentrate
1 ½ c.	¼ c.	orange juice
6 T.	1 T.	arrowroot or cornstarch
1 ½ t.	¼ t.	salt

Cook carrots covered until just tender in ½ cup water. Do not drain. **Mix** other ingredients and **add** to the carrots. **Cook**, stirring until thickened. This makes a tasty glaze over the carrots.

VEGETABLE PIE

24	8	1 c. servings

Filling:

Steam together:

6 c.	2 c.	potatoes, diced
3 c.	1 c.	green peas
3 c.	1 c.	whole-kernel corn
3 c.	1 c.	green beans
3 c.	1 c.	carrots, sliced

Gravy:

6 c.	2 c.	water
1 ½ c.	½ c.	cashew pieces
6 T.	2 T.	Vegex
3 t.	1 t.	onion powder

Blend gravy ingredients in blender until smooth. **Heat** on stove in sauce pan. **Add** (6 T.) 2 T. cornstarch dissolved in (6 T.) 2 T. water. **Heat** until thickened. **Combine** vegetables and gravy. **Place** in baked pie shell. **Top** with sesame seeds, ground.

ZUCCHINI SPECIAL

24	12	½ cup servings
8 c.	4 c.	sliced zucchini
3 c.	1 ½ c.	fresh or frozen corn
1 c.	½ c.	chopped onion
⅔ c.	⅓ c.	chopped green pepper
1 t.	½ t.	salt
2 T.	1 T.	fresh snipped dill, or
2 t.	1 t.	dried dill

Put ¼ cup water in skillet. **Add** all but salt and dill. **Cover** and **cook**, stirring occasionally for 10-12 minutes, or until vegetables are crispy done. **Add** salt and dill.

Idea—Thicken liquid to make a glaze that will enhance the flavor of the vegetables, using water and arrowroot or cornstarch.

Salads

(T) BEAN SALAD

24	12	½ c. servings
4 c.	2 c.	cooked brown rice, cold
4 c.	2 c.	kidney beans or pinto beans
2 c.	1 c.	fresh cooked or frozen corn
1 c.	½ c.	onions, sliced
2	1	medium red sweet pepper, cut into strips
1 t.	½ t.	salt or to taste
2 t.	1 t.	cumin
1 c.	½ c.	mild sauce or salsa — Pg 54
2 T.	1 T.	fresh lemon juice

Toss all and **chill.**

BEET AND WALNUT SALAD

24	12	⅓ c. servings

This tangy and unusual salad combines the wonderful nutrients of uncooked beets and nuts. It may also be served as a dip.

6 c.	3 c.	raw beets (grated)
4	2	cloves garlic (pounded or crushed in a garlic press)
3 c.	1 ½ c.	chopped walnuts
½-⅔ c.	5 T.	no-oil mayonnaise — Pg 58

Combine all ingredients lightly and serve in a glass bowl with crisp raw vegetables.

CABBAGE AND NOODLE SALAD

24	6	½ c. servings
4	1	3 oz. pkg. Oriental noodles (vermicelli)
1	¼ c.	water and ¼ t. salt
1 c.	4 T.	lemon juice (fresh)
¼ c.	1 T.	apple juice concentrate
8 c.	2 c.	finely shredded cabbage
1 c.	¼ c.	sliced green onions
¾ c.	3 T.	sesame seeds, ground
¾ c.	3 T.	almonds, sliced green pepper rings

Stir seasonings with water to dissolve and **add** to noodles, and all other ingredients except almonds and peppers. **Cover, chill** for 1-2 hours. Before serving, **stir** in almonds and **garnish** with pepper rings.

(T) CARROT PASTA

25	5	½ c. servings
5 c.	1 c.	carrots, grated (3 to 4 whole)
10 c.	2 c.	salad macaroni, cooked
2 ½ c.	½ c.	celery, chopped
1 ¼ t.	¼ t.	leaf sweet basil, crushed
2 ½ t.	½ t.	salt
2 ½ c.	½ c.	soy mayonnaise — Pg 59
5 T.	1 T.	green peppers, chopped
5 T.	1 T.	green or dry onion, chopped
1 ¼ t.	¼ t.	powdered garlic

Combine all ingredients and **mix** well. **Garnish** with salad greens, chopped parsley, and red and white radishes.

(T) CARROT SALAD

24	6	⅓ c. servings
9 ⅓ c.	2 ⅓ c.	finely grated carrots

Sprinkle with ground anise seed.

4 T.	1 T.	Peanut or Tofu Dressing, if desired.

(T) CORN RELISH

20	10	½ c. servings
4 c.	2 c.	fresh corn, cooked
4 c.	2 c.	cut green beans, cooked
2 c.	1 c.	sweet red pepper, or green, or pimiento
2	1	small onion
12 T.	6 T.	lemon juice
1 t.	½ t.	salt, to taste
1 t.	½ t.	dill weed
2 t.	1 t.	concentrate fruit juice (not necessary if corn is really sweet)

Combine well. **Chill** and serve.

CRANBERRY FRUIT SALAD

24	8	½ cup servings
3	1	can crushed pineapple in juice
1 ½ c.	½ c.	water
3 T.	1 T.	Emes gelatin
3 pkgs.	1 pkg.	fresh cranberries
½ c.	8 t.	pure cherry juice conc.
1 ½ c.	½ c.	chopped walnuts

Drain juice from pineapple. **Add** water to juice and gelatin. **Mix** well and **heat** to boil. **Add** cleaned cranberries. **Cook** 5 minutes. **Add** cherry flavor and walnuts. **Refrigerate** to set.

CRANBERRY SALAD
with Orange Dressing

30	15	½ c. servings
5 c.	2 ½ c.	boiling water
5 c.	2 ½ c.	orange juice
8 T.	4 T.	Emes gelatin
24 oz.	12 oz.	cranberries (chopped in food processor)
2	1	large orange (cut in small pieces)
2 t.	1 t.	orange peel
2 c.	1 c.	chopped sweet apple
1 c.	½ c.	chopped pecans

ORANGE DRESSING

30	15	1 T. servings
2 c.	1 c.	No Oil or Tofu Mayonnaise
4 t.	2 t.	grated orange peel
½ c.	¼ c.	orange juice concentrate

Mix well and serve on Cranberry Salad.

CUCUMBER AND POTATO SALAD

Slice equal amounts of boiled potatoes and fresh cucumber, and **blend** with delicious tofu dressing.

(T) POTATO SALAD

Slice boiled potatoes as usual. **Add** 2 medium sliced onions, 2 T. chopped parsley. **Blend** with lemon juice. **Sprinkle** with seasoning salt.

FRUIT SALAD with Lime Dressing

24	8	1 c. servings
¾ c.	¼ c.	slivered almonds
9	3	medium oranges peeled and sliced
3 c.	1 c.	grapes, seeded
6	2	medium cucumbers cut french fry style 1 ½" long
¾ c.	¼ c.	blueberries
3	1	pomegranate(s)

Combine all ingredients and **mix** with dressing.

LIME DRESSING

¾ c.	¼ c.	water
¾ c.	¼ c.	lime juice
1 ½ t.	½ t.	each curry powder (see Index) and paprika
	dash	of salt

(T) GARBANZO PASTA SALAD

25	5	1 c. servings
1 ¼ c.	¼ c.	fresh lemon juice
1 ¼ t.	¼ t.	each salt and oregano (or to taste)
15 c.	3 c.	cooked and drained pasta (large cut tubular macaroni, elbows, or shells)
10 c.	2 c.	cooked or canned garbanzos, drained
1 ¼ c.	¼ c.	each chopped parsley and diced pimiento

In medium bowl **mix** well lemon juice, salt and oregano. **Add** pasta, garbanzos, parsley and pimiento; **Toss** to mix well. **Cover**; **chill** at least 2 hours or overnight. **Season** with garlic and onion to taste. **Garnish** with roasted ground sesame seeds.

(T) GARDEN RICE SALAD

24	6	1 c. servings
12 c.	3 c.	cooked rice
2 c.	½ c.	diced cucumber
2 c.	½ c.	chopped green pepper
½ c.	2 T.	thinly sliced green onions
1 c.	¼ c.	diced pimiento
2 c.	½ c.	green onion or tofu mayonnaise

P₃57 _P₃59

Combine rice with vegetables. **Toss** lightly but thoroughly with dressing. **Spoon** mixture into a pretty glass bowl and **chill** until served. **Garnish** with cucumber slices and tomato wedges.

(T) LENTIL SALAD I

24	8	½ c. servings
12 c.	4 c.	cooked lentils
3	1	bunch green onions chopped
9	3	large tomatoes, dried small
3	1	large sweet red pepper - chopped
1 ½ t.	½ t.	cilantro (coriander leaves)
1 ½	½	can chick peas drained
¾ c.	¼ c.	lemon juice
3 t.	1 t.	salt

Mix lightly. Serve hot or cold.

(T) LENTIL SALAD II

24	4	1 c. servings
3 c.	½ c.	lentils
9 c.	1 ½ c.	water
1 ½ t.	¼ t.	salt
3 c.	½ c.	tofu
6 T.	1 T.	snipped parsley
6 T.	1 T.	tofu water
6 T.	1 T.	apple juice concentrate
¾ t.	⅛ t.	ground red peppers
12	2	small tomatoes
4 ½ c.	¾ c.	finely chopped broccoli
1 ½ c.	¼ c.	chopped green pepper
6	1	green onion(s)
6	1	dozen jumbo shell macaroni (cooked and drained)
		leaf lettuce

Cook lentils tender.

Cool slightly. **Drain,** saving liquid. **Cover** and **Chill** in the refrigerator.

Blend tofu smooth. **Stir** together tofu, parsley, apple juice, and peppers. **Cover** and **chill**.

To serve, **chop** *six (one)* of the tomato halves. **Cut** the remaining tomato into slices.

In a large mixing bowl **toss** together the lentils, tomato(es), broccoli, green pepper, and green onion. **Stir** *half* of the dressing into the lentil mixture. **Spoon** *some* of the lentil mixture into *each* cooked pasta shell. **Drizzle** with the remaining dressing. **Serve** with the tomato slices on leaf lettuce.

(T) MACARONI SALAD

24	8	½ cup servings
6 c.	2 c.	macaroni, cooked
1 ½ c.	¼ c.	chopped olives
3 c.	1 c.	shredded carrots
¾ c.	¼ c.	grated onion
3 c.	1 c.	green peas

Serve cold with White Sauce or Salad Dressing.

(T) MEXICAN BEAN AND CORN SALAD

24	8	½ cup servings
3 c.	1 c.	cooked corn
4 ½ c.	1 ½ c.	cooked and drained pinto beans
6 c.	2 c.	shredded lettuce
¾ c.	¼ c.	chopped black olives
6 T.	2 T.	peppers, green or sweet red
Dressing:		
1 ½ t.	½ t.	tomato paste
6 T.	2 T.	lemon juice
1 1 2/ t.	½ t.	cumin

(T) MILLET TABOULI

24	8	½ c. servings
1 ½ c.	½ c.	millet, toasted
4 ½ c.	1 ½ c.	water
1 ½ t.	½ t.	salt
3	1	tomato, chopped
1 ½	½	cucumber, chopped
1 ½ c.	½ c.	olives, sliced
¾ c.	¼ c.	parsley, snipped
6-9 T.	2-3 T.	lemon juice
6 T.	2 T.	green onion, chopped
1 ½ c.	½ c.	radishes, sliced

Put toasted millet in bowl, then **add** water. **Cook** until water is absorbed. **Cool** a little and **rinse** if sticky. Gently **mix** in remaining ingredients and **chill** until served.

ORANGE & VEGETABLE TOSS

24	12	1 c. servings
24 c.	12 c.	torn mixed salad greens
4	2	medium oranges, peeled & sectioned
2	1	avocado, peeled, seeded & sliced
3-4 T.	1-2 T.	lemon juice
1	½	medium cucumber, peeled, seeded, & sliced
2	1	small red onion, sliced & separated into rings
1 c.	½ c.	chopped green pepper
1 c.	½ c.	orange juice concentrate
2 c.	1 c.	tofu
2 t.	1 t.	celery seeds
½ c.	¼ c.	toasted slivered almonds

In a large salad bowl, **layer** half of the salad greens. **Add** the orange sections. **Treat** the avocado sections with lemon juice. **Layer** the avocado sections over the orange sections. Next **add** the cucumber, onion, and green pepper. **Top** with remaining salad greens. In a small bowl, **mix** the tofu and orange juice concentrate. **Spread** the mixture over the top of the salad. **Sprinkle** toasted almonds over the top. **Serve** at once!

POTATO SALAD I

24	8	½ cup servings
6 lb.	2 lb	new potatoes, cut
1 ½ c.	½ c.	**fresh** lemon juice
3 t.	1 t.	salt
3 c.	1 c.	frozen peas
2 ¼ c.	¾ c.	no oil mayonnaise —Pg 58

Cook potatoes. **Toss** while hot with lemon and salt. **Cool** and **add** peas and mayonnaise.

(T) POTATO SALAD II

24	12	½ c. servings
12-14	6-8	potatoes, cooked and cubed
2	1	medium onion, chopped
1	½	medium green pepper, chopped
6-8	4	medium carrots, grated
1 c.	½ c.	pimiento, chopped
2 c.	1 c.	mayonnaise —Pg 58 & 59
2 t.	1 t.	salt
2 T.	1 T.	lemon juice

Add chili powder (see Index) to taste. **Stir** well. **Serve** warm or chilled.

POTATO SALAD III
with Tofu Mayonnaise

24	12	½ c. servings
12	6	large potatoes
1 c.	½ c.	diced celery
1 c.	½ c.	diced green pepper
2	1	small onion, chopped
4 T.	2 T.	dill weed
2 T.	1 T.	sweet basil
½ c.	¼ c.	dill pickle, finely chopped
		salt as permitted

Mix well with tofu mayonnaise (recipe follows). **Chill** before serving.

TOFU MAYONNAISE

21 oz.	10-½ oz. pkg. regular tofu
1 ⅓ c.	⅔ c.	water
6 T.	3 T.	lemon juice
4 t.	2 t.	onion salt
2 t.	1 t.	garlic salt
2 t.	1 t.	cumin

Blend carefully all ingredients. **Garnish** with chopped parsley and radishes.

(T) SALAD
with Cumin Dressing

15	5	½ c. servings
1 ½ c.	½ c.	red pepper, yellow, green
1 ½ c.	½ c.	jicama
1 ½ c.	½ c.	carrot
1 ½ c.	½ c.	summer squash
1 ½ c.	½ c.	Cumin Dressing (follows)

CUMIN DRESSING

24	8	1 ½ t. servings
1 ½ c.	½ c.	mango or papaya or pineapple
4 ½ t.	1-½ t.	red pepper or pimiento
1 ½ t.	½ t.	each, cumin, fresh coriander, and banana pepper
3	1	small clove garlic, chopped
3	1	small shallot, chopped
4 ½ t.	1 ½ t.	date sugar
3 T.	1 T.	lime juice
¾ c.	¼ c.	chicken-like stock

Blenderize well.

(T) SALAD SIMPLE

24	8	½ c. servings
4 ½ c.	1-½ c.	peeled sliced tomatoes
4 ½ c.	1-½ c.	soft-steamed soy bean sprouts
1 ½ c.	½ c.	radish seed sprouts
¾-1 ½ c.	¼-½ c.	cashew mayonnaise —From Book 1 Pg 61
3 T.	1 T.	pineapple juice concentrate
3 T.	1 T.	lemon juice
3 T.	1 T.	finely chopped herbs
		pinch of salt

Arrange tomatoes, sprouts, and onion rings in an alfalfa sprouts lined bowl. **Mix** mayonnaise, juice, and herbs into a dressing and **pour** over the salad. **Serve** chilled.

SALAD TOSS

24	8	1 c. servings
3 c.	1 c.	16 oz. can bean sprouts, drained
3 c.	1 c.	cold cooked rice
3 c.	1 c.	chopped celery
3 c.	1 c.	coarsely shredded carrot
6 T.	2 T.	chopped green pepper
¾ c.	¼ c.	French dressing (see Index) —Pg 57
6 T.	2 T.	soy sauce
¾ T.	¼ T.	salt
1 ½ c.	½ c.	mayonnaise or salad dressing
1 ½ c.	½ c.	toasted slivered almonds (optional)

Combine all ingredients except mayonnaise and almonds; **chill**. Just before serving, **stir** in mayonnaise and almonds. **Toss** to mix well. **Serve** on leaf lettuce.

(T) TABOULI SALAD

24	8	½ c. servings
3 c.	1 c.	bulghur wheat
3 t.	1 t.	salt
3 c.	1 c.	hot water + 2 T. chicken-style seasoning
¾-1 c.	¼-⅓ c.	lemon juice
6 c.	2 c.	finely chopped fresh parsley
2 ¼ c.	¾ c.	chopped cucumber
1 ½ c.	½ c.	sliced green onions
⅓ c.	2 T.	tomatoes, chopped
1 ½ c.	½ c.	green pepper (optional)
3 c.	1 c.	cooked garbanzos (optional)

Combine first three ingredients, and **let stand** for 30 minutes. **Mix** together remaining ingredients, and **add** to wheat. **Chill**. Flavor improves upon standing.

(T) THREE-BEAN SALAD

Cooked garbanzo beans, red kidney beans, and green beans, **cut** in about 2" lengths

Celery and onion, chopped fine

Canned, sliced pimiento, diced (or diced red pepper)

Marinade: Lemon juice, and a little apple juice to achieve proper balance of tartness and sweetness. (A little water or liquid from the beans may also be added to get desired volume of liquid.)

Season with garlic and onion powder.

Toss the beans and the vegetables. **Combine** with marinade, and **mix** well. Let the bean salad sit in the **marinate** for several hours before serving, to let flavors blend. **Stir** occasionally. **Garnish** salad with onion rings.

TOFU SALAD
(Sandwich filling, cold salad)

24	8	½ c. servings
3 lbs.	1 lb.	tofu, crumbled
1 ½ c.	½ c.	mayonnaise (see Index) —Pg 58 & 59
¾ c.	¼ c.	nutritional yeast
¾ c.	¼ c.	celery, chopped fine
¾ c.	¼ c.	green pepper, fine
6 t.	2 t.	garlic powder
¾ c.	¼ c.	olives, chopped

Serve with crackers, on whole grain toast or as a hot sandwich.

(T) VEGETABLE MEDLEY

25	5	½ c. servings
10 c.	2 c.	cauliflower flowerettes
5	1	medium carrot Julienne strips
5	1	medium onion, chopped
5	1	medium green pepper, cut in one-inch squares
1 ⅔ c.	⅓ c.	pitted ripe olives

Dressing:

10 T.	2 T.	lemon juice
2 ½ t.	½ t.	dried tarragon
1 ¼ t.	¼ t.	salt
10 T.	2 T.	water

Serve cold. **Garnish** with walnut halves.

WHITE BEAN SALAD

24	4	½ cup servings
12 c.	2 c.	beans
¾ c.	2 T.	lemon juice
1 ½ t.	¼ t.	oregano
3 c.	½ c.	chopped onion
4 ½ T.	¾ T.	parsley

Mix and **refrigerate** to blend flavors.

Soups

AVOCADO CREAM SOUP

½	avocado
1 c.	chicken-like broth
1 t.	dried onion
½ t.	cumin

Blend all ingredients together for a few seconds (if too thick, **add** more broth). **Place** in saucepan; **heat** gently over low heat. **Serve** in a soup cup and **sprinkle** colorful paprika on top.

(T) BLACK BEAN SOUP

30	10	½ c. servings
6 c.	2 c.	dried black beans
3	1	tomato(es), chopped
3	1	green pepper(s), seeded and chopped
3	1	celery stalk(s), chopped
3	1	large onion(s), chopped
3 T.	1 T.	parsley
¾ t.	¼ t.	savory
¾ c.	¼ c.	milk, optional or
		nut milk or
		blend 2 c. of the beans and return
		to kettle to make a thicker soup

Cook beans in 2 ½ qt. of water. **Simmer** for 2 hours. **Add** vegetables and herbs and continue simmering 10 more minutes.

(T) BROCCOLI SOUP

24	12	1 c. servings
2	1	broccoli bunch, chopped
4	2	onions, chopped
4 c.	2 c.	celery, chopped
2 cloves	1 clove	garlic
8 c.	4 c.	rice milk
		(4 c. water—1-2 c. rice, blended smooth)
8 c.	4 c.	chick-like broth
1 t.	½ t.	thyme
1 t.	½ t.	marjoram

For a creamy soup, **blend** all ingredients smooth. **Heat** hot—do not boil.

(T) CABBAGE SOUP

24	8	½ c. servings
9 c.	3 c.	water
3 c.	1 c.	diced celery with leaves
1 ½ c.	½ c.	onion diced
1 ½ c.	½ c.	red pepper diced or pimientos
1 ½ c.	½ c.	onion diced
6 c.	2 c.	shredded cabbage (add 10 minutes before)
3 cans	1 can	water chestnuts sliced with liquid
3 cans	1 can	green beans, or use fresh or frozen
1 ½ t.	½ t.	basil
5 T.	5 t.	chicken style seasoning

Simmer 20-30 minutes.

CABBAGE SOUP

Cook in quite a bit of water:

- potatoes
- carrots
- onions
- sweet basil
- garlic
- salt
- dill
- shredded carrots (small amount)
- shredded fine, cabbage (several cups)

Prepare potatoes, carrots and onions, and **cook** in enough water to cover, plus an inch or two more. When almost cooked, **add** seasoning and **mash** a little and continue cooking. **Add** shredded carrots and cabbage. When cooked crispy, **add** cashew or almond milk and minced parsley. **Do not boil.**

This soup is really good—even the next day! Make as little or as much as you want for the occasion.

(T) CARROT SOUP

24	4	1 c. servings
12 c.	2 c.	carrots, diced
6 c.	1 c.	potato, peeled
3 t.	½ t.	salt
12 c.	2 c.	water
6 c.	1 c.	soy milk

Combine vegetables and water in a 3-qt. soup pot. Bring to a boil, **cover** and **simmer** for 15 minutes until vegetables are tender. **Puree** in a blender or processor. **Add** soy milk. **Heat** but don't boil. **Season** with parsley.

(T) CORN SOUP

24	12	1 c. servings
8 qt.	4 qt.	water
4 qt.	2 qt.	frozen corn

Heat to thaw corn. **Blend** very smooth. May need to adjust corn or water to make soup right consistency.

Add:

2 t.	1 t.	salt (or chicken-like seasoning)
2 t.	1 t.	onion powder
1 t.	½ t.	garlic powder
½ t.	¼ t.	paprika
2 c.	1 c.	parsley, fresh, chopped fine

Use the parsley for garnish.

CREAM OF GARBANZO SOUP

24	12	½ c. servings
4 c.	2 c.	cooked garbanzos, chop in blender
2 c.	1 c.	minced celery
1 c.	½ c.	minced onion
4 T.	2 T.	whole grain flour
½ c.	¼ c.	water
4 c.	2 c.	water
4 c.	2 c.	sesame milk
1 t.	½ t.	salt
½ c.	¼ c.	minced parsley
1 t.	½ t.	yeast flakes

Sauté first five ingredients until tender. **Add** remaining ingredients. (Do not boil.) May also use when recipe calls for mushroom soup.

(T) CREAM OF GREEN ONION SOUP

25	5	½ c. servings
25	5	green onions, chopped (tops and all)
12 ½ c.	2 ½ c.	water
3 ⅓ T.	2 t.	vegetable chickenlike seasoning
2 ½ c.	½ c.	mayonnaise
5 t.	1 t.	green onions, chopped

Place the water, seasonings, and green onions in blender and **puree**. Then **cook** for about 10 minutes. **Serve** in individual soup bowls. **Add** a spoonful of Tofu Sour Cream to each bowl and **garnish** with chopped onion.

CREAM OF TOMATO SOUP

24	12	1 c. servings
16 c.	8 c.	tomato puree OR
16 c.	8 c.	stewed tomatoes
2 c.	1 c.	thinly sliced celery
4	2	small cloves garlic
2-16 oz.	1 16-oz.	can(s) tomato sauce special or diced tomatoes
2 12-oz.	1 12-oz.	can tomato paste
5 t.	2 ½ t.	sweet basil
2 c.	1 c.	diced onion
1 c.	½ c.	diced green pepper
½ c.	¼ c.	red grape juice
2	1	bay leaf
		salt to taste
2 c.	1 c.	cashews (**blend** with 2 c. water until smooth) **Add** enough water to make 4 c. milk

Sauté in 1 T. water celery, onion, garlic, green pepper and bay leaf. **Heat** and **simmer** 10 minutes all tomato ingredients. **Add** celery, onion, etc. as well as seasonings and milk. Do not boil.

CREOLE PEANUT BUTTER SOUP

24	8	1 c. servings
1 ½ c.	½ c.	celery-thinly sliced
1 ½ c.	½ c.	onion-slivered
1 ½ c.	½ c.	green pepper-diced
12 c.	4 c.	water
1 ⅛ c.	⅜ c.	peanut butter
4 ½ t.	1 ½ t.	salt
1 ½ t.	½ t.	celery salt
¾ t.	¼ t.	oregano
¾ t.	¼ t.	basil
6 c.	2 c.	canned tomatoes-cut

Whiz water, peanut butter, and seasonings in blender. **Cook** together all but tomatoes until hot. **Add** tomatoes. Bring to boil. **Serve**, adding chopped parsley or chives.

DILL SOUP

24	12	½ c. servings
4	2	medium onions
2	1	green pepper
4	2	sprigs fresh dill or
2 t.	1 t.	dried seeds tied in cheesecloth
2	1	bay leaf
		sea salt to taste
2 t.	1 t.	date sugar
4 c.	2 c.	shredded cabbage
2 c.	1 c.	green beans (or wax beans)
4 c.	2 c.	tomatoes
2 T.	1 T.	flour
4 c.	2 c.	cashew milk or rice milk (T)

Sauté onions and pepper in 1 T. water. **Add** dill, bay leaf, sea salt, date sugar, cabbage, beans, tomatoes and **simmer** 20 minutes. **Remove** dill and bay leaf. **Thicken** with 1 T. flour mixed in 2 c. of cashew milk and **serve**.

(T) DRIED LIMA BEAN SOUP

24	8	1 c. servings
24 c.	8 c.	potato broth, vegetable broth or water
3 c.	1 c.	dried baby lima beans
1 ½ c.	½ c.	chopped onion
3	1	carrot, chopped
1 ½ t.	½ t.	thyme
1 ½ t.	½ t.	basil
¾ c.	¼ c.	green pepper, chopped
6	2	cloves garlic, minced or pressed
¾ c.	¼ c.	chopped parsley
		salt to taste

Simmer together broth and beans for 1 hour. **Add** onion and garlic, carrot, herbs and green pepper. **Simmer**, covered, 30 min. longer. **Puree** half the beans with some liquid, the garlic cloves and parsley. **Combine** puree with remaining soup. **Heat** to steaming. **Salt** to taste.

FRENCH ONION SOUP

20	10	½ c. servings
9 c.	4 ½ c.	water
2 T.	1 T.	beef style seasoning
4	2	medium onion-slivered or use equal amount of dry
1 t.	½ t.	savorex
		whole grain toast

Simmer first three ingredients for 20 minutes. **Spread** bread sparingly with Savorex and **put** in bottom of bowl. **Add** soup.

(T) FRESH PEA SOUP

24	6	1 c. servings
In blender **combine**:		
8 c.	2 c.	hot water
3 c.	¾ c.	cooked rice
4 T.	1 T.	onion powder
3 t.	1 t.	salt
1 t.	¼ t.	celery seed
	dash	garlic powder

Blend well. **Add** 8 c. (2 c.) fresh peas and 4 c. (1 c.) hot water. **Blend** again. **Heat** and **serve**.

(T) GAZPACHO SOUP

24	12	½ c. servings
4 c.	2 c.	vegetable or chicken-like stock
8	4	medium tomatoes, peeled & chopped
2	1	large green pepper, chopped
4	2	large cucumbers, peeled & chopped
2	1	medium onion, chopped
2	1	slice(s) whole-wheat bread, crumbled
4 T.	2 T.	lemon juice
2 t.	1 t.	ground cumin
1 t.	½ t.	salt
4	2	cloves garlic
½ c.	¼ c.	chopped pimiento

In blender **whiz** half the tomatoes until smooth. **Add** half the green pepper, cucumber and onion, the bread, lemon juice, cumin and salt. **Whiz** until smooth. **Pour** into serving bowl. **Add** the remaining tomato, green pepper, cucumber and onion, chopped fine. **Stir** into serving bowl. **Chill** at least 1 hour. May add fresh herbs: parsley, chives, basil. **Garnish** with lemon or lime slices.

(T) GREAT NORTHERN BEAN STEW

30	6	1 c. servings
7 ½ c.	1 ½ c.	Great Northern Beans (soak overnight)
5 c.	1 c.	carrots cut in large chunks
5 c.	1 c.	potatoes cut in large chunks
3 ¾ c.	¾ c.	chopped onions
3 ¾ c.	¾ c.	diced celery
1 ¼ T.	¾ t.	sweet basil
5	1	bay leaf
⅓ c.	1 T.	food yeast flakes

Cook beans until almost tender. **Add** vegetables and continue cooking until done. **Stir** well to make broth. May blend some to make a thicker soup.

(T) LEGUME SOUP

16	1 c. servings
1 c.	lentils
½ c.	pinto beans
½ c.	kidney beans
¼ c.	brown rice

Wash beans and put in large pot with about 3 or 4 quarts of water. **Simmer** slowly for 2 hours. **Add** lentils and rice.

Add:

1	large onion, chopped
½ t.	garlic
3	carrots, chopped
3	stalks celery
2	fresh tomatoes, chopped
1 t.	basil
2 t.	parsley
	Vege-Sal to taste

Cook until vegetables are done. Put in a bunch of chopped fresh spinach just before turning heat off, if desired. This keeps well and freezes great! Tastes delicious. This soup will make a hearty main dish!

(T) LENTIL BEET SOUP
with Herbed Croutons

24	6	1 c. servings
4 c.	1 c.	red lentils
4	1	large onion
8	2	medium carrots
8	2	medium beets
16-20	4-5	cloves garlic, sliced
2-4 t.	½-1 t.	salt
8	2	large bay leaves
24 c.	6 c.	water or mild stock
1 c.	¼ c.	soy sauce or equivalent
½ c.	2 T.	sesame seeds, ground

Wash and **drain** lentils, **cut** vegetables into ½" pieces. In soup pot on medium heat **put** stock, onion, carrots, beets and garlic. **Add** lentils, bay leaves, salt, and bring to a **boil**. Reduce heat and **simmer** for 1 hour, until vegetables and lentils are very soft.

Remove and **discard** bay leaves. **Add** soy sauce or Bronner's Bouillon and **puree** everything in a blender or food processor. If necessary to reheat, do so gently without boiling. **Serve** with croutons and/or other garnishes, or try it with a dollop of Tofu Mayonnaise—also good chilled!

LIMA BEAN SOUP

24	12	1 c. servings
2 lb.	1 lb.	large lima beans, dry
3 qt.	1 ½ qt.	water
1 t.	½ t.	salt
8	4	stalks celery, sliced
1 c.	½ c.	onion, large diced
½ c.	¼ c.	flour
3 c.	1 ½ c.	nut milk
		(Blend 1 ½ c. water with ¼ c. nuts)
3 c.	1 ½ c.	canned tomatoes, crushed
4 c.	2 c.	canned kernel corn, undrained
		mild sauce to taste
		salt to taste

Soak beans by preferred method. **Drain**, then **cover** with fresh water. **Cook** slowly, 1 ½ hours or until beans are tender but still holding their shape. **Add** salt. **Sauté** celery and onion in water. **Blend** in flour. **Add** nut milk. **Cook** and **stir** until thickened and smooth. **Add** beans and tomatoes and corn. **Heat** thoroughly, but do not allow to boil. **Season** to taste with mild sauce and salt.

(T) MACARONI SOUP

20	10	½ c. servings
8 c.	4 c.	hot water
6 c.	3 c.	tomato juice
2	1	bag(s) broccoli, cauliflower, carrots
1 ⅓ c.	⅔ c.	elbow macaroni
3 t.	1 ½ t.	light seasoning
1 c.	½ c.	mild sauce
2	1	can chick peas

Cook vegetables and macaroni almost done. **Add** all other ingredients. **Heat**—do not boil.

(T) MILLET SOUP

24	4	1 c. servings
24 c.	4 c.	chicken-like broth
1 ½ c.	¼ c.	millet
6 c.	1 c.	thinly sliced zucchini

In large saucepan, bring broth to a boil. **Stir in** millet. Reduce heat and **simmer** 20-25 minutes, or until millet is tender. **Add** zucchini and **simmer** 2-3 minutes or until zucchini is barely tender.

(T) ONION SOUP

24	6	1 c. servings
12	3	medium onions, sliced
5 ⅓ c.	1 ⅓ c.	cold water
⅓ c.	4 t.	yeast flakes
4 T.	1 T.	chicken style seasoning
1 c.	¼ c.	flour
2 t.	½ t.	celery salt
⅛ t.	pinch	garlic powder and thyme
13 ⅓ c.	3 ⅓ c.	boiling water

Slice onions. **Cook** in 3 ⅓ c. water. **Blend** 1 ⅓ c. cold water, ¼ c. flour and seasonings in blender. **Add** to the cooking onions. Let **simmer** 5 minutes.

PASTA GARBANZO SOUP

24	6	1 c. servings
4	1	15 oz. can(s) garbanzos with liquid or 2 c. home cooked
11 c.	2 ¾ c.	water
4 T.	1 T.	onion powder
4 T.	1 T.	chicken style seasoning
2 t.	½ t.	salt
2 c.	½ c.	soy milk powder or soy flour
6 c.	1 ½ c.	water
4 c.	1 c.	cooked whole grain pasta
4 T.	1 T.	parsley flakes
1 can	12	pitted sliced olives

Blend all but pasta, parsley, and olives. **Heat. Add** last three ingredients with garbanzos. Do not boil. Serve 1 c. each with paprika.

(T) PEA SOUP

24	8	1 c. servings
2 qts.	3 c.	frozen green peas
4 ½ qts.	1 ½ qts.	water (heat to thaw peas)

Blend above until smooth. May need to adjust peas or water to make soup right consistency.

Add:

1 ½ t.	½ t.	garlic powder
2 t.	¾ t.	onion powder
1 T.	1 t.	chicken style seasoning

Adjust to taste. **Heat** to near boiling. **Serve** with crackers, croutons, popcorn, or toast.

POTATO CREAM SOUP

24	2	1 c. servings

Put in blender:

24 c.	2 c.	water
12	1	medium potato, raw and sliced
		small handful parsley
¾ c.	1 T.	onion
¼ c.	1 t.	seasoning

Blend for 2 minutes. **Heat** for 20 minutes. If too thick, **add** more water.

POTATO SOUP

24	6	1 c. servings
12	3	potatoes, sliced thin
8	2	carrots, sliced thin
2	½	onions, sliced thin
1 c.	¼ c.	chopped parsley, fresh or dried
1 T.		sweet basil, to taste
1 T.	1 t.	chicken-like seasoning
		salt
		chopped green onions
16 c.	4 c.	water to cover

Cook above.

Add:

¼ c.	1 T.	cashews blended in
2 c.	½ c.	water

Serve hot. Do not boil.

PUMPKIN SOUP

24	4	1 cup servings
12 c.	2 c.	chicken-style broth
6 c.	1 c.	prepared pumpkin (or squash)
3 t.	½ t.	herbed seasoning
3 t.	½ t.	kelp or dulse
6 c.	1 c.	creamy nut milk
		popcorn

Peel pumpkin, **remove** strings and seeds, and **dice** into blender the required amount (1 cup). **Add** 1 cup of the chicken-style broth, and the seasoning. **Blend** until smooth and thick. Then **add** the remaining cup of chicken-like broth and nut milk. **Blend** again just until well mixed. **Heat** gently to serving temperature, **adjust** the seasoning and **serve** in warm bowls with popcorn. Serves 4.

(T) SPLIT PEA SOUP CRUNCHY OR BLENDED

24	6	1 c. servings
16 c.	4 c.	water
4 c.	1 c.	dry split peas
4	1	medium onion, chopped
4 c.	1 c.	chopped celery
4	1	clove garlic (minced) or blended in water

Cook all together until tender. For crunchy soup, **add** 1 c. (¼ c.) cooked soy grits. For blended soup, **blend** first five ingredients. No soy grits.

(T) TOMATO SOUP CREAMED

32	4	1 c. servings
32 c.	4 c.	salt free canned tomatoes and juice
2 t.	¼ t.	garlic powder
1 c.	⅛ c.	unbleached white flour
4	½	bay leaf
½ c.	1 T.	onion powder
4 c.	½ c.	soy milk
3 T.	1 t.	sweet basil

Put tomato, onion, and garlic powder, and flour in blender and **whiz** until smooth. **Pour** into sauce pan and **add** bay leaves. **Cook** over medium heat until thick, **stirring** as necessary to keep smooth. **Remove** bay leaves. Slowly **pour** soy milk into tomato mixture **stirring** as you pour. **Heat** until hot but do not boil or it may curdle. **Garnish** with minced parsley.

(T) TOMATO RICE SOUP

24	8	1 c. servings
3	1	48 oz. can(s) V-8 or tomato juice
4 ½ c.	1 ½ c.	cooked brown rice
3	1	bay leaf
1 ½ t.	½ t.	cumin (use other if you wish)

Bring to boil. **Simmer** 15 minutes.

(T) TORTILLA SOUP

24	6	1 c. servings
4 T.	1 T.	chicken style seasoning stock
8	2	corn tortillas, coarsely chopped
12	3	cloves garlic, minced
8 t.	2 t.	fresh coriander, chopped (cilantro)
2 c.	½ c.	onion, pureed
4 c.	1 c.	fresh tomato puree
6 t.	1 ½ t.	cumin powder
4 t.	1 t.	chili powder (see Index)
4	1	bay leaf
8 T.	2 T.	canned tomato puree
4 qt.	1 qt.	broth (chicken style)
1 c.	¼ c.	Worthington chicken style, cut in strips, opt.
4	1	corn tortillas in strips for garnish, toasted
1 c.	¼ c.	cubed avocado, garnish
8 T.	2 T.	cheese, garnish

Sauté first four ingredients. **Add** all ingredients reserving tortilla, avocado and cheese for garnish. **Simmer**. **Serve** with tortilla, avocado and melty cheese.

(T) VEGETABLE BARLEY SOUP

24	8	1 c. servings
2 c.	⅔ c.	barley
9	3	medium potatoes
3	1	onion
3 c.	1 c.	celery, diced
2 c.	⅔ c.	cabbage, cut small
4 ½	1 ½	qts. water
1 T	1 t.	salt
2 or 3	1	bay leaf (leaves)

Cook barley in water while preparing vegetables. **Add** all ingredients and **simmer** until tender.

VEGETABLE CHOWDER

24	6	1 c. servings
4 qt.	1 qt.	water
8 c.	2 c.	potatoes, diced
8 c.	2 c.	corn
4 c.	1 c.	tomatoes, canned
4 pkg.	1 pkg.	baby lima beans
7 c.	1 ¾ c.	sesame milk
		(1 ¾ c. water to ¼ c. sesame seeds)

Cook potatoes, limas, and corn. **Add** tomatoes. **Stir in** sesame milk. **Do not boil**. **Season** with garlic, onion and chicken-style seasonings.

(T) VEGETABLE SOUP

24	6	1 c. servings
8	2	potatoes
4	1	carrots
4	1	stalk celery
4	1	onion
4	1	green pepper
2 c.	½ c.	corn
2 c.	½ c.	peas
Seasoning:		
4 T.	1 T.	chicken style seasoning
2 t.	½ t.	onion
1 t.	¼ t.	garlic

(T) VEGETABLE SOUP II

24	8	½ c. servings
15 c.	5 c.	water (add more if needed)
6	2	potatoes, cubed
1 c.	⅓ c.	rice, cooked
1 c.	⅓ c.	cooked beans
2 medium	1 small	head cabbage, shredded
3 large	1 large	onion
3 c.	1-2 c.	beet tops
6	2	carrots, thin rounds
9 stalks	3 stalks	celery, diagonally cut thin

Cook potatoes with carrots, celery and onions. **Add** beans and rice and bring to boil. **Add** chopped beet tops and cabbage and **cook** until crispy done.

VEGETABLE TOFU SOUP

24	4	1 c. servings
18 c.	3 c.	vegetable stock or water
6	1	medium onion, sliced or chopped
6	1	clove(s) garlic, minced
6	1	medium carrot-sliced into thin diagonal rounds
6 c.	1 c.	red cabbage, sliced
24 oz.	4 oz.	tofu, cut into ½" cubes
6	1	large stalk broccoli, florets and sliced stem
12 T.	2 T.	Savita or Sovex

Optional extras: Leftover brown rice or cooked noodles, bean sprouts, etc.
Optional Garnishes: Red sweet pepper flakes, chopped green onion.

Place stock, onion, garlic, carrot and cabbage in a soup pot and **cook** over medium heat until carrot slices are tender, about 10 minutes. **Add** tofu, broccoli and any optional ingredients. When broccoli is bright green and barely tender, **remove** a cup of the broth and **stir** gradually into the Sovex or Savita in a small bowl. **Add** garnishes to soup.

VEGETABLE TOFU STEW

24	10	½ c. servings
2-3	1	large onion, sliced
3-5	1-2	cloves garlic, chopped
2 ½ lb.	1 lb.	tofu, cut into ¾" cubes
5	2	carrots, sliced
2 ½ c.	1 c.	celery, sliced
¾	¼	head(s) cabbage, chopped
3	1	summer squash or zucchini, chopped
2 ½ c.	1 c.	water
¾ c.	⅓ c.	soy sauce or equivalent
3	1	bay leaf
8 c.	3 c.	tomatoes
5	2	green peppers

Sauté in 1 T. tofu water onions and garlic, then **add** tofu and **sauté** a bit more. **Add** all except tomato and green peppers and bring to a boil, then reduce heat and **simmer**, covered, for 20-30 minutes. **Add** green pepper and tomato. If desired, **mix** some of the liquid with a few spoonfuls of flour and **cook** until thickened.

WINTER SQUASH SOUP

Cook winter squash well done. **Blend** with cooked blended soybeans and water to make right consistency. **Season** with garlic, onion, chicken-style seasoning or your choice.

SUMMER SQUASH SOUP

Cook with onion. **Blend**. **Add** beef-style seasoning and ½ as much almond milk (2 c. water to ½ c.nuts) as squash. **Add** garlic powder if desired.

(T) ZUCCHINI SOUP

24	8	1 c. servings
9 c.	3 c.	unpeeled zucchini, sliced
3	1	medium onion, diced
1 ½ c.	½ c.	celery and leaves, chopped
1 ½ c.	½ c.	diced green pepper
1 ½ c.	½ c.	finely shredded cabbage
12 c.	4 c.	water
⅓ c.	2 T.	chicken style seasoning
1 ½ c.	½ c.	hulled barley - **cook** 1 hour first.

Add all other ingredients and **cook** for additional 15 minutes.

Natural Sweets

ALMOND SWEETS

32		pieces
½ c.		orange juice
¼ c.+		dried dates
3 T.		minute tapioca

Cook together and **add:**

1 c.		walnuts, chopped fine
1 c.		coconut
3 T.		carob powder
1 c.		date sugar
1 c.		almonds, toasted, chopped fine
1 T.		vanilla

Shape in long pieces and **roll** in ground almonds. **Refrigerate.**

APPLETS

1 c.	pure apple juice concentrate
1 c.	pure apple juice
3 T.	Emes gelatin or agar agar
1 c.	chopped walnuts (medium course)
1 t.	vanilla

Mix all apple juice and thickener and **cook** until clear stirring constantly. **Add** nuts and vanilla and **pour** into a slightly oiled 9" square pan. **Sprinkle** top with finely chopped nuts or powdered macaroon coconut, or when cold **cut** into squares and roll in coconut. Let **dry** a little before storing.

APPLE CRISP

24	8	servings
3 c.	1 c.	oatmeal
¾ c.	¼ c.	sesame seeds, ground
1 ½ c.	½ c.	coconut
¾ t.	¼ t.	salt
3 t.	1 t.	coriander
3 c.	1 c.	frozen apple juice concentrate
18-24	6-8	sliced apples (medium to large)
¾ t.	¼ t.	lemon juice

Place apples in baking dish. **Mix** all the other ingredients together and **pour** over the apples. **Bake** until apples are done and crust brown.

APPLE PIE

24	8	servings
24 c.	8 c.	peeled and sliced apples
1 ½ c.	½ c.	raisins
1 ½ c.	½ c.	sunflower seeds (opt.)
3 c.	1 c.	apple juice concentrate
9 T.	3 T.	flour
3 t.	1 t.	cinnamon substitute

Combine apples, juice, raisins, flour, ground seeds and spices. **Put** in baking dish or pastry lined pie pan. **Top** with granola. **Bake** at 350° for 45-50 minutes. The oatmeal-almond crust is very good also.

APPLE NUT CAKE

24	12	servings
3 c.	1 ½ c.	date crystals
2 t.	1 t.	vanilla
3 ½ c.	1 ¾ c.	whole grain flours
1 t.	½ t.	salt
1 ½ c.	¾ c.	apple juice
2 c.	1 c.	finely chopped apples
2 c.	1 c.	walnuts, blend fine in the apple juice
1 c.	½ c.	raisins

Mix all and **bake** 30-40 minutes at 350° in prepared pan. Toothpick inserted in middle should come out clean.

APPLE PRUNE DESSERT

24	4	½ c. servings
3 c.	½ c.	pineapple juice
½ t.	⅛ t.	salt
12	2	apples, cored and cut fine
2 ¼ c.	⅜ c.	cooked pitted prunes
1 c.	8 t.	walnuts finely chopped for garnish

Whiz all but walnuts. Serve cold.

APRICOT DATE PRUNE PIE

24	8	servings
3 c.	1 c.	packed dried apricots, halved
3 c.	1 c.	packed pitted dates, halved
3 c.	1 c.	packed pitted prunes, halved
4 ½ c.	1 ½ c.	water
1 ½ t.	½ t.	salt (optional)
3	1	can (6 oz.) frozen orange juice concentrate (may use 6 oz. orange juice)
3 t.	1 t.	vanilla
3	1	pastry for two-crust 9" pie (Almond-Sesame or Oatmeal-Almond pie crust)

Put fruits, water, and salt in saucepan. Bring to **boil** over medium heat; **cover** and **simmer** until fruit is tender and water absorbed, about 10 minutes, **stirring** occasionally. **Stir** in juice and vanilla. **Chill**. **Pour** into pastry lined pie plate; **top** with lattice strips of pastry. **Bake** on bottom rack of preheated oven for 30 minutes or until crust is golden.

BAKED APPLES

24	4	one apple servings
24	4	medium sized apples
2 c.	⅓ c.	raisins
3 c.	½ c.	orange juice
3 c.	½ c.	water
¾ c.	2 T.	whole wheat flour
¾ t.	⅛ t.	salt
3 t.	½ t.	cinnamon substitute (see Index)
6 t.	1 t.	grated orange rind
3 c.	½ c.	toasted, salted sunflower seeds

Core apples without cutting through the blossom end. **Pare** the apples one-third of the way down. **Put** raisins into centers of the apples. **Place** apples in a baking dish and pour orange juice and water around them. **Combine** flour, salt, cinnamon substitute, orange rind, and sunflower seeds. **Spoon** mixture over apples, piling some in a mound on top. **Bake** at 375° about 1 hour, **basting** with the liquid every 15 minutes. The top of the filling may be toasted by placing in the broiler the last 5 minutes.

BANANA CRUMBLE
with Orange Sauce

24	8	½ c. servings
15	5	bananas, peeled and sliced
3 c.	1 c.	unsweetened crushed pineapple, drained
¾ c.	¼ c.	whole wheat flour
¾ c.	¼ c.	quick oats
¾ c.	¼ c.	walnuts or chopped peanuts
6 T.	2 T.	juice
¾ c.	¼ c.	peanut butter

Place sliced bananas in bottom of dish. **Top** with pineapple juice. **Mix** other ingredients to make crumbly mixture. **Crumble** over bananas and **bake** at 400° for 30-45 minutes.

ORANGE SAUCE
for Banana Crumble

3 c.	1 c.	tofu
1 ½ c.	½ c.	frozen orange juice concentrate

Whiz and **chill**.

BANANA DATE COOKIES

72	36	cookies
6	3	bananas mashed
2 c.	1 c.	chopped dates
1 c.	½ c.	walnut pieces
1 t.	½ t.	salt
2 t.	1 t.	vanilla
4 c.	2 c.	quick oats
2 c.	1 c.	raisins
2 c.	1 c.	coconut

Whiz all in food processor, except oats; add those last. **Drop** by tablespoon on cookie sheets. **Bake** at 350° 25 minutes.

BANANA ROLLS

Several	ripe (not overripe) bananas peeled and cut in half (not frozen)
1 c.	old-fashioned peanut butter
1 c.	dates blended with 1 c. water or chopped and cooked in water to soften
2 c.	dry cereal crumbs (Grape-nuts, shredded wheat, granola) Can be crumbed in blender

Place peanut butter in bowl and add date mixture. Gradually **stir** in crumbs adding only the amount needed to make a pliable dough that can be handled. **Pinch** off a ball of dough and **flatten** between your hands into a pancake. **Wrap** the dough around a banana and roll the wrapped banana between your hands to evenly distribute. **Roll** coated banana in coconut for a more attractive product. Place on cookie sheet and **freeze**. To serve, **slice** in ¼" slices while frozen and serve immediately. **These must be eaten frozen.** Enjoy!

BLUEBERRY DESSERT

24	12	servings
4 c.	2 c.	grape juice
2 c.	1 c.	raisins
6 T.	3 T.	arrowroot

Mix well and **cook** to thicken, then **add:**

8 c.	4 c.	blueberries, fresh or frozen

Crust:

1 c.	½ c.	date sugar
2 c.	1 c.	coconut (blended almost smooth)
4 c.	2 c.	blended quick oats
1 c.	½ c.	almonds, ground
1 c.	½ c.	flour
2 t.	1 t.	vanilla
¼ t.	⅛ t.	salt
¼ c.	⅛ c.	water (to make crumbly mixture)

Pat in 9 x 9 pan. **Bake** at 375° until brown - 20 minutes. **Pour** blueberries over and sprinkle with coconut.

CAROB TOFU PIE

24	8	⅛ pie servings
6 lb.	2 lb.	medium tofu
1 c.	⅓ c.	date crystals or dried pineapple
2 c.	⅔ c.	roasted carob powder
6 t.	2 t.	corn starch
¾ t.	¼ t.	salt
1 ½ t.	½ t.	coriander
6 t.	2 t.	vanilla
6 t.	2 t.	instant cereal coffee
2 c.	⅔ c.	hot water

Preheat oven to 350°. In a large mixing bowl, **mash** tofu and **mix** dates, carob, corn starch, salt, coriander, and vanilla. **Dissolve** cereal coffee in hot water and **mix** with tofu mixture. **Blend** in a blender until smooth—it's easier to do this in two batches. **Pour** into unbaked 9" pie crust and **bake** for about 35 minutes or until crust is done and filling has jelled.

CARROT PINEAPPLE CAKE

18	9	3" x 3" serving
1 c.	½ c.	warm water
4 T.	2 T.	yeast
1 ½ c.	¾ c.	date sugar
1 ½ c.	¾ c.	warm water
2 c.	1 c.	ground brazil nuts
8 t.	4 t.	lemon juice
4 ½ t.	2 ¼ t.	vanilla
4 ½ t.	2 ¼ t.	salt
4 t.	2 t.	grated orange peel
1 ⅓ c.	⅔ c.	soy base
1 ⅓ c.	⅔ c.	whole wheat flour
1 ⅓ c.	⅔ c.	crushed pineapple
1 c	½ c.	chopped nuts
2 ½ c.	1 ¼ c.	grated carrots
2 ½ c.	1 ¼ c.	golden flour

Dissolve yeast in water and date sugar. **Let set** 15 minutes. **Whiz** date sugar, water, brazil nuts, lemon juice, vanilla, salt and orange peel together in blender. **Add** to yeast mixture, stirring just a little. **Fold** in soy base and whole wheat flour, then the remaining ingredients in order given. **Pour** into oiled and floured 9" x 9" pan. (Should be half full.) **Let rise** 10 minutes, no longer. **Bake** at 350° until a tooth pick can be put in and brought out dry. **Serve** warm the following day. With vanilla, lemon or fresh orange sauce.

CHERRY COBBLER

24	6	servings
Filling:		
4 c.	1 c.	liquid drained from canned beets
8 c.	2 c.	thinly sliced, peeled apples
2 c.	½ c.	frozen apple concentrate
4	1	16-oz. can pitted red cherries with juice
2 c.	½ c.	water or more beet liquid
¾ c.	3 T.	corn starch
⅛ t.	Pinch	salt
3 t.	1 t.	coriander
Crust:		
3 c.	¾ c.	whole wheat flour
2 t.	½ t.	coriander powder
2 t.	½ t.	salt
2 c.	½ c.	nuts
2 c.	½ c.	water

Peel and **slice** apples and **add** with apple concentrate to beet liquid. **Cook** 20 to 30 minutes or until apples are tender. **Add** cherries and continue heating. Meanwhile **mix** remaining ingredients for filling. **Add** to cherry mixture and **stir Cook** until clear color and thick. **Pour** into 8" x 8" baking dish. Put ingredients for crust except water and nuts in small mixing bowl. **Mix** thoroughly. **Blenderize** nuts in water and **stir** into flour mixture. **Spoon** onto top of cherries. **Spread** and **bake** in preheated 400° oven for 30 minutes. **Serve** hot.

CHERRY SOUP

24	6	1 cup servings
4 qt.	1 qt.	canned dark cherries
8 c.	2 c.	pure grape juice
1 c.	4 T.	flour
½ c.	2 T.	date sugar
2 t.	½ t.	coriander
⅛ t.	Dash	salt
4 c.	1 c.	cashew cream (may add before serving)

Heat canned cherries and grape juice. **Mix** together flour, date sugar, and coriander. **Add** to cherry mixture. **Cook** to thicken. **Serve** hot or cold.

COCONUT COOKIES

96	48	1 T. cookies
2 c.	1 c.	dates
2 c.	1 c.	boiling water
1 t.	½ t.	salt
5 c.	2 ½ c.	fine coconut
4 T.	2 T.	oat flour
2 t.	1 t.	vanilla

Mix dates and boiling water. **Add** remaining ingredients. Make balls and **flatten**. **Bake** at 300° for 20 minutes.

COCONUT MACAROONS

80	2 T. cookies
1 ½ c.	pineapple or apple juice
½ c.	soaked raw soybeans
1 c.	cashews
1 c.	dates
½ t.	salt
1 T.	vanilla
1 c.	flour
5-6 c.	coconut

Blend well in blender, juice and soaked soybeans. **Add** to blender cashews and dates. **Blend** well. Then **add** to blender salt, vanilla, and flour. **Blend** again, then **pour** over coconut which has been placed in a mixing bowl. **Stir** well. Make small cookies, ½" thick. **Bake** at 325° until lightly browned.

COCONUT MACAROONS II

48	16	2 T. cookies
3 c.	1 c.	coconut
3 c.	1 c.	water
¼ t.	dash	salt
3 T.	1 T.	dried pineapple
6 T.	2 T.	oat flour
6 t.	2 t.	vanilla

Blend coconut and water until creamy. **Add** rest of ingredients, and enough coconut to hold together. **Form** small balls and **bake** at 300° for 30 minutes.

COOKIES

96	48	2 T. cookies
2 c.	1 c.	applesauce
2 c.	1 c.	date sugar
½ c.	¼ c.	any flour mixed to paste with water
2 t.	1 t.	salt
2 t.	1 t.	vanilla
4 c.	2 c.	barley flour or whole wheat
5 c.	2 ½ c.	granola or other cereal
2 c.	1 c.	nuts or sun flower seeds
		peanut butter and carob chips, opt.

Mix in order. **Drop** cookies using 2 T. per cookie. **Bake** at 325° for 15-30 minutes until crisp as you like.

COOKIES, CRISPY

4	2	dozen
2 c.	1 c.	rice flour
1 c.	½ c.	arrowroot or corn starch
1 c.	½ c.	each carob chips and nuts
⅔ c.	⅓ c.	date butter
⅔ c.	⅓ c.	apple sauce
¾ c.	⅜ c.	peanut butter
¾ c.	⅜ c.	finely ground sesame seeds or halvah
2 t.	1 t.	vanilla

Stir to mix well. **Roll** into 1" balls and **flatten** with fork. **Bake** at 375° for 15 minutes or more until light brown.

DATE BARS

1 c.	almonds, ground fine
1 c.	oatmeal
½ c.	date sugar
1 c.	coconut
	water to hold together

Mix well and **pat** ½ of above ingredients in pan. **Blend** 1 cup dates and 1 cup water for filling. **Crumble** some of the almond-oat mixture on top. **Bake** at 350° until brown in glass dish.

DATE PIE

2	large pies
3 c.	cooked brown rice
1	large banana
2 c.	boiling water
1 c.	cashews or almonds
⅔ c.	chopped dates
2 T.	carob
¼ t.	salt
1 t.	vanilla

Pour a small amount of water into blender with the nuts and **blend** until very smooth and creamy. **Add** the dates with enough water to blend well. **Add** one half of the brown rice and about one half of the remaining water; **blend** well. Then **add** the banana which has been cut into medium pieces and continue to **blend**, adding only enough water to keep your blender from pulling hard. **Stop** the blender frequently and work the mixture with a wooden spoon. **Pour** this mixture into a large bowl. **Place** the remaining rice and water in the blender with the carob and **blend** well, **add** the vanilla and salt and **pour** into the bowl with the first mixture. **Place** in refrigerator until very cold. **Put** in baked crust to serve.

DESSERT FILLING

1 c.	water
¾ t.	agar powder
1 t.	vanilla
1 ½ c.	soybean base
½ c.	blanched almonds
2-3	dates
¼ t.	salt
¼ c.	macaroon coconut

Dissolve agar in water and **boil** a few minutes. **Add** hot mixture to other blended ingredients in blender and continue to **blend** until smooth. **Chill** before using. Good with Grape-nuts or granola as a crust layered with any thickened fruit.

FRESH FRUIT PIE

24	8	1/8 pie servings
1 1/2 c.	1/2 c.	dried pineapple
9 T.	3 T.	arrowroot or tapioca
4 1/2 c.	1 1/2 c.	orange juice
3/4 c.	1/4 c.	fresh lemon juice
3 t.	1 t.	grated rind

Blend well, all except lemon juice and grated rind. Put in saucepan and **cook** until thick. **Boil** one minute. **Remove** from heat. **Add** lemon juice and rind. **Fold** in 6 cups assorted fruit for salad. Put in baked shell. **Serve** with Vitari or Banana Ice Cream.

FRUIT NUT PIE

Grind pecans to nut butter and **form crust** in pie dish. **Prepare** fresh strawberries, pineapple, fresh peaches and blueberries (any or all of your choice). **Decorate** with whole fruit and pecan halves. **Make** glaze from fruit juice concentrate by thickening 1 can juice with 1 can water and 2 T. cornstarch or arrowroot. Pie holds together better with glaze. Pecans, coconut, or carob may be added.

FRUIT PIZZA

1 1/2 c.	warm water
1 T.	dry yeast
4-4 1/2 c.	flour-whole grain
1/4 c.	ground sesame seeds

Make as for bread dough. **Roll** out on cornmeal in pizza pan or on cloth and put on sprayed pizza screen or pizza pan. **Bake** crust in 400° oven until light brown. **Cool. Mix** 1 cup drained, crushed pineapple with 2 cups tofu. **Spread** over baked crust. **Add** raspberries, raisins, sliced apples, sliced strawberries, blueberries, peaches-your choice. **Arrange** to be beautiful as well as delicious! **Heat** a few minutes and serve, or serve cold.

FRUIT SALAD

20	10	1/2 cup servings
2 2/3 c.	1 1/3 c.	honeydew melon or cantaloupe, diced
4	2	bananas
2 2/3 c.	1 1/3 c.	seedless grapes
2 c.	1 c.	raspberries or strawberries

Mix together gently.

FRUIT SALAD PARFAIT
Layered Salad with Orange Dressing

24	12	1/2 cup servings
6	3	pears, peeled, cored and sliced
4 c.	2 c.	strawberries, hulled and halved (reserve some for garnish)
6	3	peaches, peeled, pitted, and sliced
12	6	plums, pitted and sliced
4 c.	2 c.	seedless grapes, halved

DRESSING for Fruit Salad Parfait

4 c.	2 c.	soft tofu
1 c.	1/2 c.	orange juice (fresh squeezed if possible
1/2 t.	1/4 t.	almond extract
2-3 rings	1-2 rings	dried pineapple

Blend dressing ingredients until smooth. In a clean bowl **layer** fruit in five layers with dressing in dollops between layers so fruit will show through glass bowl. **Top** with dressing and strawberries. Keep **chilled** until served.

(T) GOLDEN FRUIT SOUP

24	12	1 cup servings
2 qts.	1 qt.	apricots
4 qts.	2 qts.	apricot juice
1 qt.	2 c.	pineapple
1 qt.	2 c.	fresh orange chunks
1 qt.	2 c.	banana slices

Blend apricots in apricot juice. **Add** pineapple, fresh orange, and banana slices. Serve warm or cold.

HOLIDAY DATE LOG

80	40	1/4" pieces
2 c.	1 c.	boiling water
2 c.	1 c.	chopped dates or pieces
5 c.	2 1/2 c.	very fine chopped walnuts
5 c.	2 1/2 c.	lightly chopped coconut

Blend dates and hot water to form a date butter. Place in medium size bowl. **Stir in** equal amounts of nuts and coconut until firm enough to form into a log about 1 1/2" in diameter. **Roll** log in remaining nuts and coconut. **Store** in cool, dry place for 48 hours. **Slice** into 1/4" pieces.

HOLIDAY FRUIT MOLD

Blend one 20 oz. can of unsweetened pineapple chunks. **Add** 4 rounded tablespoons of Emes gelatin (that has been dissolved in water), **heat** mixture until it simmers, then **cool**.

Puree 1 ½ c. ripe persimmons. **Add** puree to the pineapple mixture.

Add 2-4 tablespoons of frozen apple juice concentrate, with 2 cups raspberries and 2 cups frozen blueberries.

Put all into a mold and **chill** until set up. **Unmold** and **serve**.

Try using raw cranberry relish or your choice of fruit in place of the persimmons in the above recipe.

ICE CREAM

24	8	½ c. servings
1 ½ c.	½ c.	almonds
3 ¾ c.	1 ¼ c.	water
3-6	1-2	frozen bananas
6-9	2-3	dates
6 c.	2 c.	frozen raspberries or strawberries

Blend almonds and water to make a milk (no pieces of nut left). **Blend** rest of ingredients with milk in blender until smooth.

ICE CREAM II

24	6	⅔ c. servings
8 c.	2 c.	water
2 c.	½ c.	cashews or almonds
24 oz.	6 oz.	apple raspberry concentrate
8 c.	2 c.	unsweetened strawberries

Blend nuts and water until smooth. **Add** juice and berries. **Blend** and **serve** or put in freezer until time to serve.

LEMON PIE I

24	8	⅛ pie servings
9 c.	3 c.	pineapple juice

Bring juice to **boil**.

3 c.	1 c.	pineapple juice
18 T.	6 T.	arrowroot or cornstarch
6 t.	2 t.	fresh lemon juice
3 t.	1 t.	lemon extract or grated lemon peel

Stir rest of ingredients into boiling juice. **Stir** until it boils. **Remove** and **cool**. **Pour** into baked pie shell or may use crumble crust. **Decorate** with fine coconut.

LEMON PIE II

24	6	⅙ pie servings
48 oz.	12 oz.	pineapple-orange juice conc. (frozen)
1 ¼ c.	5 T.	fresh lemon juice
8 c.	2 c.	water
2 t.	½ t.	pure lemon extract
8 T.	2 T.	Emes gelatin

Dissolve gelatin in water and bring to a **boil**. **Add** other ingredients and **cool** to thicken. When set, **whiz** in blender and put in baked, cool crust and let set up again.

PIE CRUST for Lemon Pie

4	2	6 serving crusts
3 c.	1 ½ c.	oat or barley flour (blend rolled grain to make flour)
1 ½ c.	¾ c.	ground almonds
½ c.	¼ c.	ground sesame seeds
½ t.	¼ t.	salt
⅔-1 c.	⅓-½ c.	water to make soft dough

Blend nuts, seeds and salt in water until smooth. **Mix** lightly with flour dusting with oatmeal flour. **Roll** out 2 crusts and put in pie pans. **Bake** at 375° for 10-15 minutes. **Watch** carefully. Crust should be slightly brown. **Cool** before adding the cooled lemon filling.

If you wish a stronger flavor of lemon, just **add** ¼ of the lemon peel or less and **blend** when you blend all the other ingredients.

(T) MELONS
with Lime Dressing

24	12	½ c. servings
1	½	small watermelon, make balls
2	1	Casaba melon, make balls
2	1	Crenshaw melon, make balls
2	1	large cucumber, peel, score outside, thinly slice

Mix above gently in bowl.

2	1	large head(s) of lettuce

Line watermelon shell with ruffled lettuce around top. Hold in place with toothpicks.

LIME DRESSING
for Melons

1 ⅓ c.	⅔ c.	fresh lime juice
1 c.	½ c.	dried pineapple, **blend** smooth in juice
1 t.	½ t.	poppy seeds

Add poppy seeds. **Drizzle** over top of salad.

OATMEAL CARROT COOKIES

4	2	dozen
4 c.	2 c.	rolled oats
1 c.	½ c.	coconut, unsweetened
1 c.	½ c.	chopped nuts
½ c.	¼ c.	flour
2 t.	1 t.	vanilla
1 t.	½ t.	salt
2 c.	1 c.	finely grated carrots
⅔ c.	⅓ c.	dates, blended or date sugar

Pack grated carrots loosely in measuring cup. **Fill** to top with water. **Combine** carrots, water, and date sugar. **Add** the remaining ingredients, mixing well. **Drop** from teaspoon onto a prepared or non-stick cookie sheet and **bake** at 350° for 20 minutes.

(T) ORANGE JULIUS

10	2	servings
3 ¾ c.	¾ c.	water and
1 ¼ c.	¼ c.	soy milk powder blended or
5 c.	1 c.	Eden Soy Milk
1 ¼ c.	¼ c.	frozen orange juice concentrate
5	1	fresh orange
1 ¼ t.	¼ t.	vanilla
20	4	ice cubes to thicken

Whiz in blender and serve.

PANCAKES OR CREPES

100	25	crepes
12 c.	3 c.	water
2 lbs.	8 oz.	tofu
8 c.	2 c.	rice flour
2 t.	½ t.	salt
1 c.	¼ c.	raw almonds
¼ c.	1 T.	apple juice concentrate
2 c.	½ c.	oatmeal

Put all ingredients in blender except oats. **Add** enough oats to make thin batter. **Blend** thoroughly. **Stir** before making each pancake or crepe. **Serve** with fruits or vegetables.

PEACH ALMOND TART

24	8	1 c. servings
Crust:		
2 ¼ c.	¾ c.	whole wheat pastry flour
2 ¼ c.	¾ c.	rolled oats
1 ½ c.	½ c.	ground almonds
6 T.	2 T.	date sugar

Mix in food processor or by hand. **Put** half of mixture on the bottom of a 9 x 9 pan.

Filling:		
18 c.	6 c.	sliced peaches
6 t.	2 t.	lemon juice
1 ½ c.	½ c.	date sugar
4 ½ T.	1 ½ T.	whole wheat pastry flour or oat flour
3 t.	1 t.	grated lemon rind
3 t.	1 t.	natural almond flavor

Layer ½ of peaches and then other ingredients, the rest of peaches and the rest of other ingredients. **Sprinkle** crust mixture on top. **Bake** at 350° until bubbly.

(T) PEACHY FRUIT SHAKE

24	4	½ c. servings
15 c.	2 ½ c.	very ripe sliced peaches, frozen
3	½	ripe banana
3 c.	½ c.	apple juice
⅓ t.	1/16 t.	each, vanilla and almond

Blend ingredients in blender until smooth and no crystals remain. **Serve** immediately.

PEANUT BUTTER CAROB BROWNIES

45	15	3" x 2 ½" servings
3 c.	1 c.	peanut butter
2 ¼ c.	¾ c.	whole wheat pastry flour
1 c.	⅓ c.	carob powder
¾ t.	¼ t.	salt
1 ½ c.	½ c.	date sugar
3 t.	1 t.	vanilla

Preheat oven to 350°. Have all ingredients at room temperature for best results. **Mix** flour, carob powder, salt, peanut butter, date sugar, and vanilla. **Spread** batter into prepared 9 x 13 baking pan. A rubber spatula is helpful—wet it to smooth out the top. **Bake** at 350° for 18-20 minutes. **Cool** and **cut** into squares.

PEANUT BUTTER COOKIES

48	16	cookies
2 c.	2/3 c.	peanut butter
5 1/4 c.	1 3/4 c.	oat flour (add last)
3/4 c.	1/4 c.	date sugar
3/4 c.	1/4 c.	water
3/4 t.	1/4 t.	salt

Shape into small balls. **Flatten** with fork moistened in water. **Bake** at 350° for 30 minutes or until brown and crisp.

PEANUT BUTTER OATIES

24	8	2 cookie servings
6 c.	2 c.	ground oatmeal
3 c.	1 c.	date sugar
3 c.	1 c.	raisins
3 c.	1 c.	chopped pecans
1 1/2 t.	1/2 t.	salt
1 1/2 t.	1/2 t.	cardamon
1 1/2 t.	1/2 t.	coriander

In double boiler **heat** and **mix** ingredients below with ingredients above.

3 c.	1 c.	peanut butter
3 c.	1 c.	water
3/4 c.	1/4 c.	orange juice concentrate
2 T.	2 t.	vanilla flavoring
1 T.	1 t.	lemon flavoring

Bake 15 minutes at 375° or 20 minutes at 300°.

PEANUT CRUNCH CLUSTERS

24	8-10	1/4 c. servings
36 oz.	12 oz.	carob bits, unsweetened
1 1/2 c.	1/2 c.	peanut butter, smooth or crunchy
6 c.	2 c.	dry roasted peanuts, coarsely chopped

Melt carob bits and peanut butter in top of double boiler over hot water. **Stir in** peanuts. **Drop** by teaspoonfuls on waxed paper.

PECAN BARS

24	12	servings
2	1	recipes almond-oat crust
2 c.	1 c.	soy milk
2 t.	1 t.	salt
4 t.	2 t.	vanilla
3 c.	1 1/2 c.	pecans
6 T.	3 T.	arrowroot or cornstarch
1 1/3 c.	2/3 c.	date crystals

Mix all in blender except nuts. **Chop** nuts and **add** to mixture. **Pour** into almond-oat crust in baking dish. **Put** 1/2 c. pecan halves on top to decorate. **Bake** 1 hour at 325°.

PIE CRUST SUGGESTIONS

Lighter crusts or crackers can be made by blending in a blender until smooth, the nuts, seeds and water. These can be your choice but the amount should be 1/2 to 3/4 as much as the flour for a tender, crisp product.

The flour used may be any whole grain, any mixtures of grains, but the oat, barley and rice will make a lighter product. Use a variety for best results. Flour may have to be adjusted. Dough should not be sticky.

PIE CRUST I

6	2	pie crusts
4 1/2 c.	1 1/2 c.	rice flour
3 c.	1 c.	oat flour
2 1/4 c.	3/4 c.	sesame seeds
1 1/2 c.	1/2 c.	water
1 1/2 t.	1/2 t.	salt

Blend smooth sesame seeds and water. **Mix** all ingredients gently. **Roll** out between plastic.

PIE CRUST II

6	2	pie crusts
3 c.	1 c.	barley flour
3 c.	1 c.	oat flour
3 c.	1 c.	almonds
1 1/2 c.	1/2 c.	water
3/8 t.	1/8 t.	salt

Blend smooth almonds and water. **Mix** all ingredients together. If making crackers, add 1 1/2 c. cornmeal and 1/2 c. walnuts. **Roll** directly on cookie sheet with plastic on top. **Score. Bake** at 250° until crunchy.

PIE CRUST ALMOND SESAME

6	1	8 serving pie crusts
2 c.	1/3 c.	almonds (ground)
2 c.	1/3 c.	sesame seeds (ground)

Whiz above ingredients in blender with 1/2 c. water until smooth. Put the following in a bowl and **mix** well.

3 c.	1/2 c.	whole wheat flour
3 c.	1/2 c.	barley flour, or
6 c.	1 c.	barley flour or oat flour in place of above flours
2 c.	1/3 c.	full fat soy flour, opt.
1 T.	1/2 t.	salt

Add blended mix to dry ingredients, **mix** well and **knead** lightly. Dough should not be sticky. If so, **add** a little more flour. **Roll** between wax paper until very thin (about 1/16"). **Prick** with fork. **Bake** at 375° until golden brown. Walnuts or pecans can be substituted for almonds.

PINEAPPLE COCONUT DESSERT

24	4	1/2 c. servings
4 1/2 c.	3/4 c.	juice from 6(1) can(s) crushed pineapple plus water
1 1/2 c.	1/4 c.	frozen orange concentrate
4 1/2 c.	3/4 c.	almonds
3 t.	1/2 t.	vanilla
3/4 c.	2 T.	cornstarch
6 cans	1 can	pineapple
2 1/4 c.	6 T.	coconut
3/4 c.	2 T.	walnuts

Combine juice and water to make desired amount. Place in blender. **Add** to blender orange juice concentrate, almonds, vanilla, and corn starch. **Cook** until thick. **Add** pineapple and coconut. Place in serving dish and **sprinkle** with walnuts.

PINEAPPLE PIE FILLING

24	8	servings
3	1	20 oz. can(s) crushed unsweetened pineapple
6 T.	2 T.	arrowroot or cornstarch
3/4 c.	1/4 c.	water

Put pineapple in saucepan and bring to **boil**. **Dissolve** corn starch in water and **add** to pineapple. **Cook** until thickened. **Cool**. **Fold** in 1/2 to 3/4 c. cashew cream. **Pour** into baked pie shell.

PINWHEEL DATE COOKIES

48	12	cookies
16 c.	4 c.	whole wheat pastry flour
2 t.	1/2 t.	salt
4 c.	1 c.	ground walnuts
4	1	6 oz. can(s) frozen orange juice
4 t.	1 t.	water
8 t.	2 t.	vanilla

Mix dry ingredients. **Blend** smooth in blender, walnuts, orange juice, water, and vanilla. **Add** liquid to the dry ingredients and **mix** only enough to moisten flour. **Divide** into three balls. **Roll** out to 1/4" thick rectangle between two sheets of plastic. Use 1/3 of filling—spread over dough. **Roll** up and **seal**. **Wrap** in plastic wrap. **Freeze** until used. **Cut** in 1/4" slices. **Bake** at 350° 8-10 minutes. **Fillings follow:**

DATE APRICOT FILLING
for Pinwheel Date Cookies

48	12	cookies
2 c.	1/2 c.	chopped apricots
6 c.	1 1/2 c.	pitted dates
1 c.	1/4 c.	undiluted apple juice concentrate
3 c.	3/4 c.	pecans or almonds, finely chopped

Blend all except nuts. **Cook** to thicken. **Add** nuts.

DATE ORANGE FILLING
for Pinwheel Date Cookies

48	12	cookies
8	2 c.	pitted dates
4	1 can	6 oz. frozen orange juice, undiluted
2 c.	1/2 c.	water
3 c.	3/4 c.	pecans finely chopped

Blend all except nuts. **Cook** to thicken. **Add** nuts.

DATE LEMON FILLING
for Pinwheel Date Cookies

48	12	cookies
6 c.	1 1/2 c.	pitted dates
3 c.	3/4 c.	hot water
1/4 c.	1 T.	lemon rind or
4 t.	1 t.	lemon flavoring
6 t.	1 1/2 t.	coriander (ground)
8	2	drops anise
3 c.	3/4 c.	walnuts or pecans finely chopped

Blend all except nuts. **Cook** to thicken. **Add** nuts.

PEANUT BUTTER COOKIES

48	16	cookies
2 c.	⅔ c.	peanut butter
5 ¼ c.	1 ¾ c.	oat flour (add last)
¾ c.	¼ c.	date sugar
¾ c.	¼ c.	water
¾ t.	¼ t.	salt

Shape into small balls. **Flatten** with fork moistened in water. **Bake** at 350° for 30 minutes or until brown and crisp.

PEANUT BUTTER OATIES

24	8	2 cookie servings
6 c.	2 c.	ground oatmeal
3 c.	1 c.	date sugar
3 c.	1 c.	raisins
3 c.	1 c.	chopped pecans
1 ½ t.	½ t.	salt
1 ½ t.	½ t.	cardamon
1 ½ t.	½ t.	coriander

In double boiler **heat** and **mix** ingredients below with ingredients above.

3 c.	1 c.	peanut butter
3 c.	1 c.	water
¾ c.	¼ c.	orange juice concentrate
2 T.	2 t.	vanilla flavoring
1 T.	1 t.	lemon flavoring

Bake 15 minutes at 375° or 20 minutes at 300°.

PEANUT CRUNCH CLUSTERS

24	8-10	¼ c. servings
36 oz.	12 oz.	carob bits, unsweetened
1 ½ c.	½ c.	peanut butter, smooth or crunchy
6 c.	2 c.	dry roasted peanuts, coarsely chopped

Melt carob bits and peanut butter in top of double boiler over hot water. **Stir in** peanuts. **Drop** by teaspoonfuls on waxed paper.

PECAN BARS

24	12	servings
2	1	recipes almond-oat crust
2 c.	1 c.	soy milk
2 t.	1 t.	salt
4 t.	2 t.	vanilla
3 c.	1 ½ c.	pecans
6 T.	3 T.	arrowroot or cornstarch
1 ⅓ c.	⅔ c.	date crystals

Mix all in blender except nuts. **Chop** nuts and **add** to mixture. **Pour** into almond-oat crust in baking dish. **Put** ½ c. pecan halves on top to decorate. **Bake** 1 hour at 325°.

PIE CRUST SUGGESTIONS

Lighter crusts or crackers can be made by blending in a blender until smooth, the nuts, seeds and water. These can be your choice but the amount should be ½ to ¾ as much as the flour for a tender, crisp product.

The flour used may be any whole grain, any mixtures of grains, but the oat, barley and rice will make a lighter product. Use a variety for best results. Flour may have to be adjusted. Dough should not be sticky.

PIE CRUST I

6	2	pie crusts
4 ½ c.	1 ½ c.	rice flour
3 c.	1 c.	oat flour
2 ¼ c.	¾ c.	sesame seeds
1 ½ c.	½ c.	water
1 ½ t.	½ t.	salt

Blend smooth sesame seeds and water. **Mix** all ingredients gently. **Roll** out between plastic.

PIE CRUST II

6	2	pie crusts
3 c.	1 c.	barley flour
3 c.	1 c.	oat flour
3 c.	1 c.	almonds
1 ½ c.	½ c.	water
⅜ t.	⅛ t.	salt

Blend smooth almonds and water. **Mix** all ingredients together. If making crackers, add 1 ½ c. cornmeal and ½ c. walnuts. **Roll** directly on cookie sheet with plastic on top. **Score. Bake** at 250° until crunchy.

PIE CRUST ALMOND SESAME

6	1	8 serving pie crusts
2 c.	1/3 c.	almonds (ground)
2 c.	1/3 c.	sesame seeds (ground)

Whiz above ingredients in blender with 1/2 c. water until smooth. Put the following in a bowl and **mix** well.

3 c.	1/2 c.	whole wheat flour
3 c.	1/2 c.	barley flour, or
6 c.	1 c.	barley flour or oat flour in place of above flours
2 c.	1/3 c.	full fat soy flour, opt.
1 T.	1/2 t.	salt

Add blended mix to dry ingredients, **mix** well and **knead** lightly. Dough should not be sticky. If so, **add** a little more flour. **Roll** between wax paper until very thin (about 1/16"). **Prick** with fork. **Bake** at 375° until golden brown. Walnuts or pecans can be substituted for almonds.

PINEAPPLE COCONUT DESSERT

24	4	1/2 c. servings
4 1/2 c.	3/4 c.	juice from 6(1) can(s) crushed pineapple plus water
1 1/2 c.	1/4 c.	frozen orange concentrate
4 1/2 c.	3/4 c.	almonds
3 t.	1/2 t.	vanilla
3/4 c.	2 T.	cornstarch
6 cans	1 can	pineapple
2 1/4 c.	6 T.	coconut
3/4 c.	2 T.	walnuts

Combine juice and water to make desired amount. Place in blender. **Add** to blender orange juice concentrate, almonds, vanilla, and corn starch. **Cook** until thick. **Add** pineapple and coconut. Place in serving dish and **sprinkle** with walnuts.

PINEAPPLE PIE FILLING

24	8	servings
3	1	20 oz. can(s) crushed unsweetened pineapple
6 T.	2 T.	arrowroot or cornstarch
3/4 c.	1/4 c.	water

Put pineapple in saucepan and bring to **boil**. **Dissolve** corn starch in water and **add** to pineapple. **Cook** until thickened. **Cool**. **Fold** in 1/2 to 3/4 c. cashew cream. **Pour** into baked pie shell.

PINWHEEL DATE COOKIES

48	12	cookies
16 c.	4 c.	whole wheat pastry flour
2 t.	1/2 t.	salt
4 c.	1 c.	ground walnuts
4	1	6 oz. can(s) frozen orange juice
4 t.	1 t.	water
8 t.	2 t.	vanilla

Mix dry ingredients. **Blend** smooth in blender, walnuts, orange juice, water, and vanilla. **Add** liquid to the dry ingredients and **mix** only enough to moisten flour. **Divide** into three balls. **Roll** out to 1/4" thick rectangle between two sheets of plastic. Use 1/3 of filling—spread over dough. **Roll** up and **seal**. **Wrap** in plastic wrap. **Freeze** until used. **Cut** in 1/4" slices. **Bake** at 350° 8-10 minutes. **Fillings follow:**

DATE APRICOT FILLING
for Pinwheel Date Cookies

48	12	cookies
2 c.	1/2 c.	chopped apricots
6 c.	1 1/2 c.	pitted dates
1 c.	1/4 c.	undiluted apple juice concentrate
3 c.	3/4 c.	pecans or almonds, finely chopped

Blend all except nuts. **Cook** to thicken. **Add** nuts.

DATE ORANGE FILLING
for Pinwheel Date Cookies

48	12	cookies
8	2 c.	pitted dates
4	1 can	6 oz. frozen orange juice, undiluted
2 c.	1/2 c.	water
3 c.	3/4 c.	pecans finely chopped

Blend all except nuts. **Cook** to thicken. **Add** nuts.

DATE LEMON FILLING
for Pinwheel Date Cookies

48	12	cookies
6 c.	1 1/2 c.	pitted dates
3 c.	3/4 c.	hot water
1/4 c.	1 T.	lemon rind or
4 t.	1 t.	lemon flavoring
6 t.	1 1/2 t.	coriander (ground)
8	2	drops anise
3 c.	3/4 c.	walnuts or pecans finely chopped

Blend all except nuts. **Cook** to thicken. **Add** nuts.

PRINCESS PUDDING

24	6	½ c. servings
8 c.	2 c.	unsweetened pineapple juice
2 c.	½ c.	pineapple juice
⅛ t.	pinch	salt
2 c.	½ c.	cornmeal
4	1	banana (not too ripe)
2 T.	1 ½ t.	vanilla
1 c.	¼ c.	coconut
		your favorite granola

Cook cornmeal in 2 c. pineapple juice. **Blend** ½ c. pineapple juice, banana, coconut, vanilla and salt until smooth. **Pour** freshly cooked cornmeal into blender with other ingredients and **blend** until smooth. **Put** layer of granola on bottom of dish, layer granola with banana then pour banana cream mixture in dish. May garnish with sliced fresh strawberries.

RASPBERRY SAUCE AND RICE PUDDING

24	8	servings

The Raspberry Sauce:

3	1 can	apple raspberry concentrate
3	1 can	water

Thicken with arrowroot or tapioca. **Cool.** Gently **add:**

3	1 pkg.	raspberries. Set aside.

The Rice Pudding:

9 c.	3 c.	cooked rice
1 ½ c.	½ c.	fruit juice concentrate
1 ½ t.	½ t.	salt
3 c.	1 c.	nut milk
2 T.	2 t.	vanilla

Bake rice mixture to heat thoroughly. **Serve** with raspberry sauce.

RHUBARB CREAM PIE OR PUDDING

1	unbaked pie crust
	cashew pie filling
	diced rhubarb

Bake at 450° for 40-45 minutes or until set.

(T) RHUBARB STRAWBERRY COBBLER

24	8	1 c. servings
12 c.	4 c.	rhubarb, 1" pieces
3 ¾ c.	1 ¼ c.	crushed pineapple
7 ½ t.	2 ½ t.	arrowroot or cornstarch
12 c	4 c.	fresh strawberries, or
12 c.	4 c.	frozen strawberries
3 c.	1 c.	golden raisins

Layer rhubarb, strawberries and raisins in baking pan. **Mix** arrowroot with pineapple and **pour** over rhubarb layer.

COBBLER DOUGH

Blend:

> ½ c. warm water
> 2 T. yeast
> 6 dates

Then **add:**

> 2 c. warm water
> 2 t. salt
> 1 t. orange grated
> ½ c. orange juice concentrate
> 6 ¾ c. flour plus enough to make soft dough

Make into jelly roll. **Cut** and **lay** on top of rhubarb and strawberries. **Bake** at 350° for 30-45 minutes or until fruit is bubbly and bread is baked.

*One recipe is enough for 24 servings.

RHUBARB PINEAPPLE CRISP

24	8	½ c. servings
3 c.	1 c.	nuts, ground
4 ½ c.	1 ½ c.	dates or date sugar
4 ½ c.	1 ½ c.	oatmeal
1 ½ c.	½ c.	flour
2 ¼ t.	¾ t.	salt

Mix above ingredients well. It will be crumbly. Use half for bottom, half for top.

3 c.	1 c.	rhubarb
6 c.	2 c.	crushed pineapple in own juice
2 ¼ c.	¾ c.	pineapple juice concentrate
¾ t.	¼ t.	salt
¾ c.	¼ c.	cornstarch or arrowroot
3 t.	1 t.	lemon juice

Cook to thicken. **Put** together with above mixture in baking dish and **bake** 30-40 minutes at 350°.

RICE FRUIT PUDDING

30	10	½ c. servings
6 c.	2 c.	cooked, salted rice
¾ c.	¼ c.	raisins
3 c.	1 c.	drained, crushed pineapple
3 T.	1 T.	vanilla
2 ¼ c.	¾ c.	hot liquid (pineapple juice and water)
¾ t.	¼ t.	salt
¾ t.	¼ c.	raw cashew pieces
¾ t.	¼ c.	frozen orange concentrate
3	1	banana

Mix rice, raisins, pineapple and vanilla. **Blend** liquid, salt, cashews, orange concentrate and banana. **Mix** all together carefully. **Serve** with 1 tsp. raisins for garnish for each person.

TAPIOCA PUDDING

25	5	½ c. servings
1 ½ c.	5 T.	tapioca
2 ½ c.	½ c.	dried pineapple chunks
10 c.	2 c.	pineapple in its own juice
1 ⅔ c.	⅓ c.	cashews or almonds
⅝ t.	⅛ t.	salt
5 t.	1 t.	vanilla

Blend dried pineapple chunks, pineapple in juice, nuts and salt until smooth in liquefier. **Add** tapioca just before turning off. **Cook** over medium heat to a full boil, **stirring** constantly—6-8 minutes. **Stir** in vanilla. **Cool** 20 minutes. **Stir.** **Serve** warm or chilled. **Fold in** crushed pineapple, raspberries or sliced peaches or garnish as desired. Good as a filling for crepes with crushed strawberries over the top.

TOFU CHEESECAKE

24	8	servings
6 lbs.	2 lb.	tofu
1 ½ t.	½ t.	salt
¾ c.	¼ c.	lemon juice
1 ½ c.	½ c.	dried pineapple
2 T.	2 t.	vanilla
3 T.	1 T.	cornstarch
9 T.	3 T.	water
3 ¾ c.	1 ¼ c.	granola, crumbed

Preheat oven to 350°. **Prepare** crust by crushing granola in blender to make 1 ¼ c. crumbs. **Press** into 9" pie plate. **Blend** rest of ingredients to make filling. **Pour** filling into crust and **bake** for 40 minutes or until top is golden-brown and cake has jelled. Let **cool** before serving, or **chill** if desired. **Top** with sliced fresh fruit.

TOFU DELIGHT

24	8	½ c. servings
3	1	block(s) tofu
5	1-2	bananas
6-9 T.	2-3 T.	either orange or pineapple juice concentrate
3 T.	1 T.	vanilla
3	1	bag(s) frozen strawberries can substitute frozen peaches with almond extract

Blend in blender until smooth. **Serve** in sherbet glasses with coconut sprinkled on top.

TOFU PUMPKIN PIE

24	8	⅛ pie servings
4 ½ c.	1 ½ c.	tofu
3	1	16 oz. can pumpkin
3 t.	1 t.	salt
3 t.	1 t.	vanilla
1 ½ t.	½ t.	coriander
3 c.	1 c.	date butter or equivalent
3 t.	1 t.	vanilla
1 ½ t.	½ t.	orange rind

Pour into unbaked pie shell. **Bake** at 350° for 1 hour or until baked in center. **Serve** plain or with creamy topping.

Miscellaneous

BATTER FOR BREADING
(eggplant, zucchini, etc.)

1 c.	water
½ c.	chick pea flour, to thicken to batter
¼ c.	fresh, or ½ t dried onion, pepper, chives savory salt, to taste

Blend smooth in blender.

BREAD MAKING

Water in bread gives a crusty bread with a good wheaty flavor. Try adding 1 T. lemon juice for each 3 c. flour for a lighter, more tender crumb. Use wheat flour high in gluten for large, light loaves. If gluten is low, add 1-2 T. gluten flour for each cup of flour. Nuts, seeds, and sprouted grains can be added for additional nutrients.

One teaspoon of diastatic malt is all that is needed for 4 or 5 loaves of bread for sweetener. Diastatic malt is sprouted wheat that has been dried and ground to a powder. Dry the sprouts in a food dryer or in oven set at 150° or less. Sweeteners feed the yeast and provide flavor, tenderness, crispness and browness.

Salt is not necessary for bread making but it does regulate the growth of the yeast. Breads made without salt may rise very rapidly and fall during baking.

Flours are not all the same in moisture content. Some require more water than others. When adding flour keep back a little until you know you need all of it.

BREADING MEAL I

When you pop corn in the air popper some of the kernels do not pop and there are always bits and pieces of corn in the bottom of the serving bowl. Sometimes the corn has been sprayed with salt and sprinkled with food yeast. Put all left over in nut grinder and grind fine. Use for patties, or whenever you need crumbs or breading meal.

BREADING MEAL II

½ c.	whole wheat flour
½ c.	cornmeal
¼ t.	each salt, onion powder, garlic thyme, celery powder, dried yeast (omit any you do not enjoy)

CANNING FRUIT

Wash fruit and core or pit (peaches should be peeled; peelings can be left on all other fruits.) Blend in blender with no added liquid, enough fruit to yield 1 ½ c. puree. Add 1 t. lemon juice and stir. Put puree in clean quart jar and add slices of same fruit to fill jar. Stir slices into puree so there is mixed puree and slices up to within ¾" of top of jar. (Do not add any water or juice.) Prepare enough jars in same manner to fill canner.

Wipe tops of jars carefully. Place lids in boiling water for 1-2 minutes to soften rubber. Lift out with magnetic lifter. Put lids on jars and screw rings on firmly. Put jars in canner and cover with water. (I recommend a steam canner. Ask me about this terrific canner.) Bring to boil and boil gently about 20 minutes. Remove from canner and cool in draft-free location. Do not tighten rings after processing.

CRUMBLY CHEESE

4	1	cup(s)
2 c.	½ c.	food yeast food
2 c.	½ c.	sesame seeds ground
4 t.	1 t.	garlic powder
4 t.	1 t.	onion powder
4-8 t.	1-2 t.	chicken seasoning
¼ c.	3 t.	lemon juice

Combine. Mix well. Put in closed container. Keeps for weeks in refrigerator.

HERBED WHOLE WHEAT CROUTONS

24	6	cups
24	6 slices	whole wheat bread, cut in cubes
¼ c.	1 T.	soy sauce or equivalent
2 t.	½ t.	each oregano, sage, thyme
1 t.	¼ t.	garlic powder

Cut bread into cubes. Combine rest of ingredients in mixing bowl. Toss cubed bread in this mixture to coat well. Spread on baking dish and bake for 15-20 minutes at 350° until light brown and crispy.

LEGUMES—COOKED,
comparison of some nutrients

1. SOYBEANS   1/2 cup   4. WHITE BEANS 1/2 cup
2. GARBANZOS   1/2 cup   5. RED BEANS   1/2 cup
3. LENTILS   1/2 cup   6. SPLIT PEAS   1/2 cup

approximate:

	1	2	3	4	5	6
Calories	130	130	106	118	118	115
Protein	11.0	8.1	7.8	7.8	7.8	8.0
Fat	5.7	1.0	trace	.6	.5	.3
Carbohydrate	10.8	22.1	19.3	21.2	21.4	20.8
Calcium	73	60	25	50	38	11
Phosphorus	179	135	119	148	140	89
Iron	2.7	2.8	2.1	2.7	2.4	1.7
Potassium	540	320	249	416	340	296
Vitamin A	30	20	20	0	trace	40
Thiamine	.21	.13	.07	.14	.11	.15
Riboflavin	.03	.06	.06	.07	.06	.09
Niacin	.6	.8	.6	.7	.7	.9
Ascorbic Acid	0	0	0	0	0	0

Values based on *Agriculture Handbook* No. 8

MASA HARINA AMERICANIZED

1 dozen tortillas

To make the dough, you will need 1 ½ c. of corn flour, 1 ½ c. of sifted whole wheat flour, ½ c. ground nuts, and about 1 ¼ c. of water. **Mix** all the ingredients together, **knead** until smooth—adding more flour if necessary. **Form** the dough into balls about 1 ½" in diameter. **Roll out** the tortillas from the balls, or make in tortilla press. **Bake** them on a hot dry griddle until bubbles turn brown on each side.

MELTY CHEESE

12	3	cups
16 oz.	4 oz. jar	pimientos
½ c.	2 T.	arrowroot or cornstarch
2 c.	½ c.	cashew nuts
1 qt.	1 c.	water
8 t.	2 t.	salt
1 c.	¼ c.	food yeast
1 c.	¼ c.	oatmeal (quick preferable)
½ c.	2 T.	lemon juice
4 t.	1 t.	onion powder
6 c.	1 ½ c.	boiling water

Blenderize all except boiling water. **Add** to boiling water and **cook** until thick. **Serve** warm on tacos, haystacks, corn chips or use on pizza, lasagna, etc.

NOODLES

Use extra fine stone ground flour, or finely **grind** your own flour. Take 2 cups of flour and **add** just enough water to get it together. (The stiffer the dough, the better, as there is that much less moisture to evaporate.) When the dough is in a lump, let it **stand** for a while. (About an hour so the moisture will have a chance to penetrate and make the dough smoother and evenly moistened.) Then **roll out** to a very thin thickness; the thinner the better. Do not add salt; **use** only flour and water. When dough is rolled out **place** same on the cloths and let it **dry** for an hour or so, then **cut** into strips two inches wide. **Pile** the strips on top of each other and **cut** them up to any desired width. To cook, **Put** them in salted boiling water. If noodles are to be stored, **sprinkle** with some stone ground flour and **mix** it with cut noodles. **Dry** noodles perfectly and they will keep in a dry place a long time.

NOODLES BUCKWHEAT

½ t.	sea salt
1 ½ c.	buckwheat flour
½ c.	whole wheat flour
½ c.	soy flour
½ c.	cold water
	extra flour for rolling

Mix salt into flours with your hands in a shallow bowl or use bread maker. **Add** the water slowly—how much depends upon the dryness of the flour, etc. Dough should be soft but not wet.

Knead well for 10 minutes or until the dough is elastic. **Pat out** on a well-floured board and **roll** from the center outward, trying to keep the dough uniformly thick. When it becomes fairly thin, **dust** the surface with flour and **roll** around a chopstick. **Remove** chopstick and **slice** cross wise into thin strips. **Cook** in boiling water for 10 minutes and **drain**. **Serve** with a sauce or in soups. May store if thoroughly dry.

24 HOUR PICKLES

4	1	quarts
1 qt.	1 c.	boiling water
1 ⅓ c.	⅓ c.	lemon juice
2 t.	½ t.	onion powder
2 t.	½ t.	garlic powder
1 t.	¼ t.	celery seed

Wash and **slice** cucumbers into jar. **Put** fresh onion and garlic pieces in jar along with dill (if available). **Pour** above mixture over and let **stand** 24 hours before serving. Good in potato salad, sandwiches, or serve as pickles.

Soymilk and Okara—How to Make

This recipe makes 1 gallon of soymilk and ½ gallon of okara.

Soak 2 ½ cups of raw soybeans for 12 hours, changing the water every 3 or 4 hours in warm weather. Soybeans ferment quickly, so if a foam develops on the surface of the water, don't panic, as the legumes are still usable. Just skim the foam off the top, rinse the beans, and proceed. (The batch will yield a slightly thinner milk, that's all.)

After 12 hours, strain the beans. Add 1 cup of the soaked legumes to 2 ½ cups of fresh warm water in a blender, and whirl it at high speed for 30 seconds. Continue to puree the rest of the beans—using the same proportions—until all of the legumes have been liquefied. Then cook this mash in a heavy covered pot on medium-low heat, stirring frequently, until it begins to boil. Turn the heat down to low and let the liquid simmer slowly for 45 minutes. Stir the slow-cooking mash every 5 minutes or so to prevent it from boiling over.

Next, remove the soy slurry from the stove and set the pot in a sink containing cold water. Keep the water around the pan chilled until the milk is just warm. (The more quickly soymilk cools, the longer it will keep.) As soon as the mix reaches a "touchable" temperature, strain it through a clean cloth. An old cotton pillowcase will do, but nylon chiffon works very well. It is dense enough to prevent the mash from seeping through, but thin enough to allow the milk to flow.

Close the top of your cloth and begin twisting it to force the juice through the bag. When you have little more than a mushy ball left, squeeze gently so as not to force any pulp through the fabric.

Bottle the strained milk in sterile glass jars. Milk remains fresh for approximately a week when it's kept in several small containers that are used one at a time.

Now, dump your okara into a small plastic bucket or wide-mouthed glass jar. The mash also keeps for about a week in the refrigerator. It's sweetest and best in dessert dishes the first 3 to 5 days. After that, it tends to get a slight tang and tastes better in yeast breads, or Mexican corn bread. If you have any remaining after a week, compost it. Okara is an excellent soil amendment, but, like any bean product, it ferments strongly. Therefore, sprinkle the meal thinly into your garden or compost.

OKARA. *Oh-kar'-ah.* The name is unfamiliar to most people in the United States, but it ought to be more well-known than apple pie! Nutty-flavored, low in fat, and high in protein and fiber, this versatile bean meal is possibly the most nutritious *and* inexpensive food available to the American consumer today.

Okara is a by-product of the making of all soy "dairy" foods. After the soaked beans are ground to a fine mash, cooked in water, and strained, they yield soymilk and okara in a 2:1 ratio. In commercial operations, the creamy liquid is used to make bean ice cream, soy yogurt, and tofu, but the nutritious meal is frequently given away as livestock feed.

People who cook with soybeans commonly dry the strained meal (may be dried in food drier or oven), grind it into flour, and use it as we do wheat flours (although okara contains no gluten).

Okara can be added to breads, cereals, and desserts. The unsung soy food—which, when dried and ground, can substitute for up to half the flour in baked goods—blends right in, contributing (in addition to nutritional value) moistness and perhaps a touch of nutlike flavor.

Now it's your turn to experiment! Remember that okara may be added to almost any yeast or quick bread to provide fiber, protein, and a subtle, nutty taste. The mash makes a perfect burger or loaf extender. The soy milk can be used wherever a recipe calls for milk.

Sprouting Mung Beans*

1. Place a tablespoon of seeds in a large-mouth jar, cover with water and let soak 8 to 12 hours.

2. Cover the neck of the jar with cheesecloth or nylon netting secured with a rubber band. May also use nylon screen with jar ring.

3. Pour off the "soak" water (this is excellent for your houseplants).

4. Rinse the seeds with warm water and leave the jar tilted with the mouth down.

5. Rinse and drain each morning and night (more often if temperature is high) until sprouts reach the desired length.

6. NOTE: **Mung beans become bitter if the sprouts turn green** so, unlike most sprouts, keep them away from sunlight.

* For more on sprouting, see *Cooking With Natural Foods, Book I.*

WAYS TO USE MUNG BEAN SPROUTS:

Add to vegetables; add to tossed salad; use in coleslaw; use in potato salad; use in lasagna, stir into chickpea a la king; stew with tomatoes; sauté with onions; puree with peas or beans; substitute for Chinese vegetables; braise with celery; stuff with corn into peppers; stir into soups and stews at the last moment; add to any Chinese or Japanese dish; use in stuffed cabbage or grape leaves; use on sandwiches in place of lettuce.

Seasonings

BEEF LIKE SEASONING

3 c.	1 ½ cups	
2 c.	1 c.	nutritional food yeast
6 T.	3 T.	sweet pepper flakes
6 T.	3 T.	parsley flakes
6 T.	3 T.	salt
3 T.	4 ½ t.	dill seed
3 T.	4 ½ t.	onion
2 T.	1 T.	basil
2 t.	1 t.	rosemary
2 t.	1 t.	thyme

Put all ingredients into the nut and seed grinder or blender. **Blend** fine.

CHICKEN-LIKE SEASONING

4	2	cups
3 c.	1 ½ c.	nutritional yeast
5 t.	2 ½ t.	sweet pepper flakes
2 T.	3 t.	onion
5 t.	2 ½ t.	salt
5 t.	2 ½ t.	rubbed sage
5 t.	2 ½ t.	celery seed
5 t.	2 ½ t.	garlic
5 t.	2 ½ t.	thyme, ground
2 ½ t.	1 ¼ t.	marjoram
2 ½ t.	1 ¼ t.	tarragon
2 ½ t.	1 ¼ t.	paprika
2 ½ t.	1 ¼ t.	rosemary, ground

Blenderize fine.

CHICKEN-LIKE SEASONING II

2 ½	1 ¼ cups	
1 c.	½ c.	salt
1 c.	½ c.	food yeast
2 T.	1 T.	soy flour
⅔ c.	⅓ c.	onion powder
2 T.	1 T.	cumin
1 T.	½ T.	garlic
1 ⅓ t.	⅔ t.	marjoram or thyme
1 ⅓ t.	⅔ t.	sweet basil
1 T.	½ T.	paprika
4 T.	2 T.	parsley flakes

Whiz all ingredients except parsley flakes until very fine. **Add** parsley flakes and **whiz** briefly.

CHILI POWDER SUBSTITUTE

1 c.	3 T.	
⅔ c.	2 T.	paprika
5 T.	1 T.	parsley flakes
5 t.	1 t.	ground oregano
5 T.	1 T.	dried bell pepper (green or red)
5 t.	1 t.	dill seed
2 ½ t.	½ t.	savory
1 ¼ t.	¼ t.	garlic powder
10	2	bay leaves
5 t.	1 t.	cumin
5 T.	1 T.	sweet basil
5 t.	1 t.	onion powder

Put all ingredients together and **grind** to fine powder in nut and seed mincer. Good for flavoring beans.

Another Chili Substitute - Spanish onions with cumin.

CHILI SEASONING

1 ⅓	cups
6 T.	oregano
3 T.	thyme
3 T.	sweet basil
2 T.	cumin powder
8 T.	parsley flakes

Whiz in blender.

CURRY SEASONING

1 T. each   ground bay leaf, celery seed, cumin, coriander, fenugreek, and onion powder

HERB SEASONING
for Croutons or Crumbs

10	2 ½	*cups seasoned bread crumbs*
20	5 slices	whole wheat bread
1 c.	¼ c.	food yeast
4 t.	1 t.	dried oregano, crushed
4 t.	1 t.	dried basil, crushed
4 t.	1 t.	dried thyme, crushed
4 t.	1 t.	dried marjoram, crushed
4 t.	1 t.	dried parsley flakes
2 t.	½ t.	dried rosemary, crushed
2 t.	½ t.	dried savory, crushed
2 t.	½ t.	salt
2 t.	½ t.	celery seed
2 t.	½ t.	fennel seed
2 t.	½ t.	paprika
2 t.	½ t.	ground sage
1 t.	¼ t.	garlic powder

Place 2 ½ slices bread in a blender container. **Cover** and **blend** fine. Empty blender. **Blend** 2 ½ more slices. **Blend** herbs and **add** to crumbs.

ITALIAN HERB SEASONING

Almost 1 c.

4 T.	oregano
4 T.	rosemary
2 T.	basil
2 T.	marjoram, ground
2 T.	thyme, whole
½ t.	sage, rubbed
1 t.	garlic granules

Place in blender and **blend**.

SEASONED SALT

2 c.	1 c.	(almost)
1 ½ c.	¾ c.	salt
2 t.	1 t.	each thyme leaves, marjoram, garlic powder or granules, cumin, celery salt, onion powder
4 t.	2 t.	paprika
2 t.	1 t.	each chives, parsley
½ t.	¼ t.	dill seed

Blend in blender or seed grinder. **Store** in glass jar.

SWEET HERB SEASONING

2 ¼ cups

1 c.	cornmeal (non-degerminated or whole, ground fine) Also grind popcorn that doesn't pop.
⅔ c.	onion powder
1 T.	garlic powder
1 ½ t.	thyme (whole ground)
1 T.	paprika, mild
1 ½ t.	sweet basil (dried, ground)
2 T.	parsley (dried, ground)
⅓ c.	salt (omit for therapeutic diet)

Combine ingredients and **mix** well. **Store** in airtight container in cool, dry place.

VEGETABLE BROTH POWDER

1 ½ cups

1 T.	dried parsley
2 T.	dried green bell pepper
1 T.	dried red bell pepper
1 T.	celery seed
4 T.	onion powder
1 c.	food yeast

Mix together and **whiz** up in Moulinex grinder. Other dried vegetables can be added to this to get different flavors.

Some Seasoning Alternatives

Basil—Sweet basil is a favorite in tomato dishes. The delicate taste enhances spreads, dressings, casseroles, soups, and salad dressings.

Celery—Because celery is naturally rich in sodium, it is a good choice for a salt-free novice. Both the seeds and leaves add zip to cole slaw, potato salad, cooked vegetables, tomato dishes, dressing, tofu, stews, and soups.

Coriander—The seeds of this hardy annual may be added to cookies, pies, rolls, fruit crisps, etc., and also bean dishes.

Cumin—This seed is a common ingredient in chili, pickles, and bean dishes. The unique flavor grows on one the more it is used.

Dill—Chop it into garden salads, spreads, potato salad, soups, and stews. Dill seeds add a fresh flavor to breads, tofu, legume dishes, and bean salads.

Fennel—Both the seeds and leaves taste pleasantly of licorice. Use it in entrees, green salads, cream soups, potatoes, beets, and pastries.

Garlic—In salad dressings, soup, dips, sauces and Italian recipes, garlic can't be beat. Add it finely minced to all types of legumes and vegetable dishes.

Marjoram, sweet—This attractive herb tasting of thyme (only stronger and sweeter) is most versatile. Include it in vegetables, soups, stews, salad dressings, and green salads.

Mint—Add a touch of mint to new potatoes and peas. Also use it sparingly in bean and lentil dishes, eggplant, casseroles, carrots, split pea soup and Mid-East dishes.

Oregano—As a salt replacer, oregano ranks high. Use it in pizza and lasagna sauce, bean soup, and vegetables.

Paprika—Add this herb, loaded with vitamins A and C, to stews, sauces, soups, green vegetables, potato salad, and cole slaw.

Parsley—Add lots of this bright green vitamin C giant to sauces, dips, salad dressings, breads, tofu, soups, and vegetables. Parsley is a good breath sweetener.

Rosemary—Include it in pasta sauce, tomato dishes. Use it lightly with rice, herb bread, dumplings, dressing and peas.

Sage—is strong flavored. It peps up bean soup, tofu, bread dressings and some casserole dishes.

Savory, summer—Its biting flavor goes with stuffing, beans and peas, tofu dishes, and dressings.

Tarragon—Essential to "fines herbes"; it helps relieve salt-craving. Add it to soups, herb spreads, salad dressings, beets, green beans, celery, potatoes, and tomato dishes.

Thyme—This herb has an affinity for soup, tomato juice, spaghetti sauce, stew, stuffing, tofu, and most vegetables.

Further suggestions:

Parsley has long been a favorite with carrots. Try adding a little caraway seed or garlic along with the parsley.

Green peas may be given a different flavor by adding basil, mint or thyme.

Spinach may be seasoned with most herbs, but is especially good with basil or garlic.

Summer squash goes well with celery seed, basil, thyme, or toasted sesame seed.

Zucchini has a delicious flavor when cooked with tomato, onion, celery and green pepper. Be sure to season this combination with a little garlic and Italian seasoning.*

Green beans taste good with sesame and/or poppy seeds or seasoned with dill or basil.

Broccoli will have a change of flavor when you season with dill, basil, marjoram, celery seed, or caraway seed.

Pasta sauce—basil, thyme, rosemary may be added in equal parts.

Soup, tofu, and **stews**—thyme, summer savory, rosemary used in equal parts or 3 parts thyme, 3 parts parsley, 1 part cumin, 1 part sage.

Note: Be sure to use only small amounts of herbs when introducing them to your family. **Too much** can't be taken out.

*Italian seasoning is a combination of herbs used in Italian cooking that may be purchased at any spice counter.

From Other Countries

Chinese

CASHEW SUB GUM

4	servings
4 oz.	bean sprouts
½ c.	bamboo shoots
1	4 oz. can water chestnuts, diced
½	green pepper, diced
½ c.	cashew nuts, slightly roasted
2	green onion, diced
¾ c.	celery, diced
¼ c.	pimientoes, chopped
1 t.	date sugar
1 T.	soy sauce
1 T.	cornstarch

Stir-fry green onions, celery, green pepper, bamboo, and water chestnuts for 3 minutes. **Add** pimiento, date sugar, soy sauce, and cornstarch which has been mixed with small amount of water. **Turn** over twice with spatula. **Remove** to serving dish. **Top** with cashews. Recipe serves 4 as a main dish. If desired, blanched almonds may be substituted for the cashews.

EGGLESS FOO YUNG

3 c.	water
⅔ c.	dry soybeans
	(**soak** overnight and then **drain** and **blend** in 1 ¼ c. water)

Add:

1 ¼ c.	rolled oats
1 c.	chopped onion
1 t.	Italian seasoning
2 T.	chicken-style seasoning
2 T.	Aminotone or soy sauce
1 ½ c.	mung bean sprouts, slightly chopped

Cook all but sprouts until soybeans are well done—30 to 40 minutes. **Add** sprouts and **cook** 5-8 minutes.

PEANUTS (Main dish)

peanuts
garlic powder
soy sauce
Five star seasoning (Chinese anise)

Soak peanuts overnight. **Cook** until done, **adding** seasonings, or **place** in pressure cooker and **add** seasonings. Bring to **boil** and when it starts ringing **turn off** and time 20 minutes of pressure in pan without removing lid or pressure gauge. **Serve** with brown rice, Chinese vegetables, rolls and avocado spread, **Cream** with bananas and black cherries and pinch of coconut.

TOFU CANTONESE

24	6	½ c. servings
8 lb.	2 lb.	tofu in pieces
4 t.	1 t.	each garlic salt and paprika
4	1	large onion, sliced
6	1 ½	large green peppers, cut in thin strips
4 c.	1 c.	diagonally sliced celery
5 c.	1 ¼ c.	chicken-style broth
½ c.	2 T.	cornstarch
¾ c.	3 T.	soy sauce or equivalent
8	2	large fresh tomatoes, cut in eighths
12 c.	3 c.	hot cooked rice

Cut tofu in thin strips. **Sprinkle** with seasonings. **Saute** 1 to 2 minutes in non-stick pan. **Add** onion, green peppers, celery, and ½ c. broth. **Cover; steam** 2 minutes. **Blend** remaining broth with cornstarch and soy sauce. **Stir** into tofu mixture. **Add** tomatoes; **cook** and **stir** 2 minutes or until sauce is slightly thickened. **Serve** over beds of fluffy brown rice.

FALAFELS

1 c.	dry garbanzos, soaked over night, or for at least 4 hours
1	small onion, chopped
1	clove garlic, chopped
1 or 2	sprigs parsley
1 t.	salt
2 t.	chicken-like seasoning (See recipe)
1 t.	cumin
⅓ c.	cornmeal
¼ c.	sesame seeds

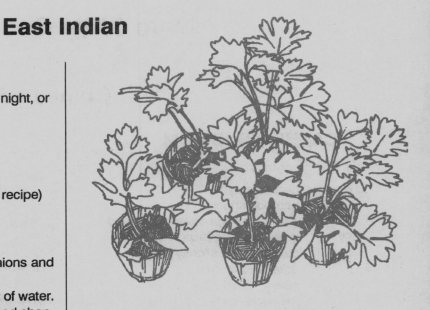

Toppings: Diced cucumbers, tomatoes, green onions and lettuce.

Sort garbanzos, **wash** and **soak** in about a quart of water. **Drain. Grind** 1 ⅓ c. soaked garbanzos through food chopper (using medium-fine blade) or **chop** in food processor. **Whiz** remaining soaked garbanzos (about ⅔ c.) in blender with ⅓ c. water, onion, garlic and parsley leaves (discard the stems); **add** all remaining seasonings: **blend** well. Shape into walnut-size balls. **Bake** on pan at 350° for 30 minutes. **Serve** in pocket bread with above toppings.

Greek

DILL CARAWAY POTATO SOUP

24	6	servings
12	3	large potatoes, sliced into 1" cubes
4	1	medium leek, chopped
4	1	medium carrot, chopped
4	1	stalk celery, chopped
14 c.	3 ½ c.	vegetable stock or water
4-8 c.	1-2 c.	milk-soy or nut
2 ⅔ T.	2 t.	dill weed
2 t.	½ t.	caraway seeds
2 c.	½ c.	plain tofu blended with lemon
1 ⅓ c.	⅓ c.	chopped fresh parsley

Place vegetables and stock or water in a large soup pot. **Cook** over medium heat, covered, until potatoes are tender, about 20 minutes. **Pour** soup into blender in two batches and **blend** just until smooth. **Return** soup to pot, **add** enough milk for desired consistency, then **add** the dillweed and caraway seeds. **Heat** soup a few minutes more. Just before serving, **stir in** tofu but do not boil. (Remember not to boil soup when reheating.) **Garnish** with parsley.

Suggested meal additions: Green salad, warm muffins, nut butter.

(T) GREEK LENTIL SOUP

24	8	1 c. servings
6 c.	2 c.	uncooked lentils, rinsed
24 c.	8 c.	water
1 ½ c.	½ c.	chopped onion
3	1	small carrot(s), diced
3	1	medium potato(s), diced
6 T.	2 T.	chicken-like seasoning
1 T.	1 t.	salt
6	2	bay leaves (remove before serving)
3	1	celery stalk(s), diced or sliced
3 T.	1 T.	lemon juice

Simmer all ingredients together, except lemon juice, about 30 minutes. **Add** lemon juice just before serving.

GREEK TOFU SCRAMBLE

4	servings
1	medium onion, diced
1	small green pepper, diced
½ c.	diced Jerusalem artichoke or eggplant
1 lb.	regular tofu, mashed
1 t.	each oregano and basil, crumbled
¼ t.	salt
½ c.	melty cheese (See Index)
1	medium tomato, sliced
2 T.	chopped fresh parsley

Sauté onion and pepper until onion is soft in a little water. **Add** artichoke or eggplant and continue cooking until softened. **Add** mashed tofu and seasonings and **mix** well. **Pour** tofu mixture onto sautéed vegetables and **cook** over medium heat, covered, for a few minutes. **Turn** mixture over and **cook** 2 to 3 minutes longer. **Dribble** cheese onto mixture. **Garnish** with tomato and parsley. **Serve** immediately.

Suggested meal additions: Steamed broccoli, toast or crusty loaf of warm bread.

LENTIL BURGERS

24	12	½ c. servings scant
6 c.	3 c.	cooked lentils
1 c.	½ c.	diced onion
1 c.	½ c.	diced celery
2	1	bay leaf

Add the onion, celery and bay leaf to the lentils during last ten minutes. **Remove** from heat and **remove** bay leaf.

Add:

2 T.	1 T.	tarragon
4 t.	2 t.	marjoram
2 t.	1 t.	ground cumin
1 t.	½ t.	lemon juice
1 t.	½ t.	salt
1 ½ c.	¾ c.	rolled oats
1 ½ c.	¾ c.	whole grain bread crumbs

Shape into patties. **Bake** at 400° for 15 minutes or until lightly brown.

POLENTA SUPPER

1 c.	yellow cornmeal
½ t.	salt
4 c.	water
2 c.	thick, Italian-style tomato sauce
⅔ c.	grated pizza cashew cheese

Mix the cornmeal with one cup of cold water until blended. **Bring** the remaining three cups of water to a boil in a heavy saucepan. **Add** salt, then **stir in** the conrmeal paste and return to a boil, stirring continuously. **Reduce** heat to low and **simmer**, stirring occasionally with a wooden spoon, until the mixture is very thick. **Add** a little water, if needed. **Cook** 15-20 minutes, depending on how fine or coarse the cornmeal is. When ready to serve, **stir in** half of the cheese, then **spoon** into bowls and **top** with hot tomato sauce and remaining cheese. **Serve** with green salad, warm bread.

Variations: Omit cheese and top with hot chili beans, or stir-fried vegetables and a spoonful of melty cheese.

Italian

CREAMY TOMATO SAUCE

Serve over cooked fettucini noodles.

4	servings
¼ c.	mayonnaise
½ c.	tofu with lemon and salt
1 ½ T.	tomato juice
1	14-oz. can artichoke hearts (in water)
	fresh chopped parsley for garnish

Blend in blender mayonnaise, tofu and tomato juice until smooth. **Drain** artichokes and **rinse** well under cold water. **Cut** artichokes into halves or quarters and **stir into** sauce. **Heat**—do not boil. To serve, **pour** sauce over pasta and **garnish** with parsley before serving.

FIFTEEN MINUTE TOMATO SAUCE

2	servings
1	large garlic clove, minced
1	large green pepper, cut into thin strips
3 c.	tomato juice or puree
1 t.	oregano
1 t.	basil

Sauté garlic and green pepper in 1 T. water for about 3 minutes, until garlic begins to color. **Stir in** tomato juice or puree and seasonings. Bring to a boil and **simmer**, uncovered, for 10 minutes. **Serve** over warm pasta.

Variation: For a more substantial sauce, **add** 2 cups of coarsely chopped cooked kidney beans or tofu cubed. **Simmer**.

(T) GAZPACHO

24	12	½ c. servings
6	3	clove garlic, diced fine
1 c.	½ c.	green pepper, diced fine
½ c.	¼ c.	onion, diced fine
2	1	cucumber, diced
2	1	tomato, diced
6 T.	3 T.	lemon juice
8 c.	4 c.	tomato juice
½ t.	¼ t.	cumin
		salt to taste

Combine all ingredients and **serve** cold.

ITALIAN EGGPLANT

4-6	servings
1	medium eggplant
1 c.	almond milk
½ c.	fine zwieback crumbs
¼ c.	flake yeast
¼ t.	salt
1 c.	spaghetti sauce
1 T.	oregano
1 c.	cashew cheese

Slice eggplant in ½" slices. **Dip** in almond milk and then in crumbs and yeast mixture. **Place** on prepared baking sheet. **Spoon** spaghetti sauce and cashew cheese on top each slice and **sprinkle** with oregano. **Bake** at 450° for 10-20 minutes.

LENTIL SAUCE

6-8	servings
1	large clove garlic
1	medium onion, chopped
½ lb.	(about 1 ¼ c.) raw lentils, cleaned
3 c.	water
1 t.	salt (omit if tomatoes are salted)
½ t.	oregano
7-8	fresh basil leaves OR
¼ t.	dried basil
¼-½ t.	sweet dried red pepper or
1-2"	piece mild banana pepper, sliced
2 c.	chopped tomato (fresh, frozen, or canned)
4-6 T.	tomato paste

In a 2- to 3-quart pot put garlic, onion, lentils and water. Bring to a boil, **cover**, and **simmer** over low heat for about 30 minutes. **Add** seasonings and chopped tomato to lentil mixture. **Cook** another 20 minutes, or until lentils are tender. **Add** 4 T. tomato paste and **simmer** gently, uncovered, for 5 minutes, until sauce begins to thicken. **Add** remaining 2 T. tomato paste if necessary to make a thicker sauce. **Serve** sauce over warm pasta.

PEANUT BUTTER SAUCE for Pasta

6	servings
1 c.	chopped onion
1 c.	slivered green pepper
1 c.	warm water
½ c.	peanut butter
4	tomatoes, diced
3 c.	tomato juice
1 t.	oregano
2 T.	coarsely chopped peanuts

Sauté onion and green pepper in water for about 5 minutes, until wilted. In separate pan, **stir** water gradually into peanut butter until smooth; **add** onion and green pepper mixture along with tomatoes, tomato juice and oregano. Bring a boil, stirring occasionally until sauce is smooth. To serve, **spoon** hot sauce over cooked pasta and **top** with chopped peanuts.

PERFECT PASTA AND SAUCES

Pasta is convenient. Pasta keeps indefinitely at room temperature and goes from box to table in about 10 minutes. Pasta is economical. A pound of pasta can feed four to eight people. Pasta is as nutritious as the flour from which it is made. Whole-grain pasta has fiber, vitamins, and minerals. Pasta has variety with many sauces. It can be simple or elaborate according to the sauces. Make whole-grain pasta a more frequent addition to meals.

PESTO

4	servings
¼ c.	pine nuts or sunflower seeds, mixed with a few walnuts
½ c.	crumbly cheese (See Index)
2 c.	fresh basil (lightly packed) or a combination of basil and parsley. Or
2 T.	if dried. Crush to bring out flavor.
¼ t.	salt
2	cloves garlic, crushed
2-3 T.	melty cheese (optional)

Finely **grind** nuts in a food processor or blender. **Add** crumbly cheese, herbs, salt and garlic and **puree** to a thick paste. (If using the blender, it may be necessary to stop and push mixture down several times.) **Blend** until the sauce is smooth and creamy. **Serve** over warm pasta. **Pass** melty cheese.

SALSA

2 c.	tomato sauce
2 c.	chopped tomatoes
1 c.	chopped onion
1 c.	each chopped green pepper and red pepper
4	cloves fresh garlic—minced salt to taste

Serve on hot pasta.

SPAGHETTI OR LASAGNA SAUCE

2	#2 ½ cans tomatoes
1 t.	salt
2 T.	parsley
1 t.	oregano
½ t.	garlic powder
1	large green pepper
½ t.	thyme
½ t.	rosemary
½ t.	celery seed
½ t.	basil
½ t.	cumin

Simmer and **add:**

1 c.	fresh cooked zucchini
4 c.	cooked lentils

Blend.

SWEET RED PEPPER SAUCE

4-6	servings
2	large red peppers, sliced
1	large onion, sliced or chopped
1	16 oz. jar pimientos, drained
1 c.	water
1 T.	lemon juice
½ t.	date crystals
3 T.	minced parsley or
1 T.	dried parsley
1 t.	dried oregano
1 t.	dried basil

Sauté peppers and onion until until translucent. **Puree** pimientos with water in a blender or food processor until pulpy. **Pour** pimiento puree and remaining ingredients into the pot with the onion and simmer for 5 minutes. **Serve** over hot pasta.

Mexican

BLACK BEAN CHILI

2 c.	dried black beans
1	bay leaf
3	medium onions, peeled, sliced
4	large garlic cloves, peeled
1	mild banana pepper
½ t.	salt
2 t.	ground cumin
3 t.	dried oregano
2 t.	paprika
2 lb.	canned tomatoes
1 T.	lemon juice
¼ c.	cilantro leaves, opt.

Preparation time about 15 minutes.

Sort and **rinse** beans well. **Cover** with water in a large pot and **soak** overnight or 1-2 hours. **Drain** beans, **cover** with fresh water and bring to the boil. **Add** bay leaf, **reduce** heat and let beans simmer. When almost cooked, **add** other ingredients. **Cook** until beans are soft and other ingredients well done. **Chop** onions coarsely. **Heat** 1 T. water in large skillet over medium heat; **sauté** onions, stirring frequently until soft, 5-7 minutes. **Chop** garlic and mild banana pepper finely. **Add** to skillet with herbs and **cook** 5 minutes. **Drain** tomatoes; **reserve** juice. **Chop** coarsely. **Add** to skillet with reserved juice and **simmer** 15 minutes.

Add skillet mixture to beans. Continue cooking slowly until thick and beans are soft, about 1 ½ hours. **Add** lemon juice and **season** to taste. **Chop** cilantro finely. **Add. Serve** with optional garnish.

CHAPPATIS

8	*5" chappatis*
1 c.	whole wheat flour
1 c.	corn flour
⅛ t.	salt
1 c.	cold water (just enough to keep dough from sticking to hands)

Divide into 8 portions. **Roll** out thin. **Toast** on medium-high dry skillet or griddle about 30 seconds on each side.

CORN TORTILLAS

1 c.	cooked corn (blend in ½ c. water)
4 c.	corn flour
2 c.	whole wheat flour
½ T.	salt
1 ½ T.	yeast, baker's

Dissolve yeast in warm water and make a dough. **Roll** out thin and **bake** on dry griddle, or make in tortilla maker.

ENCHILADAS

12	*cups*
1	tortilla
¼ c.	beans
¼ c.	sauce
1 T.	onion

Dip tortilla in sauce and put beans and onion inside. **Pour** remainder of sauce over roll. **Bake** at 350° for 1 hour.
Take 4 of 8 cups cooked pinto beans and **blend** with juice from cooking the beans. **Stir** back in with whole beans. (24 servings)

Sauce:

7 c.	tomato puree
2 c.	canned tomatoes, blended
2	onions, chopped
2	cloves garlic
2 ¼ t.	cumin
½ t.	oregano
2	bell peppers, chopped
1 T.	garlic powder

Simmer several hours.

GARBANZO DIP

25	*2 T. servings*

A zippy Garbanzo dip (Mexican Chick Peas) served with crackers or corn chips.

1	1 lb. can garbanzos
1 c.	minced onion
½ t.	oregano
2 T.	minced parsley
3 T.	pine nuts, pistachios, or other nuts, ground

Drain garbanzos with enough of the liquid to put in blender and **blend** smooth. **Cook** onion in water until tender. **Add** to mixture parsley, nuts, and oregano. **Stir** well. **Spoon** into serving bowl, **cover** and **chill**. **Sprinkle** with toasted ground sesame seeds, and serve as dip with chips or crackers. Makes about 3 cups.

MEXICALI CASSEROLE

2 pkg.	tofu—14 oz. each
2	28 oz. mild taco sauce
2 T.	chili powder (See Index)
2	8 oz. tomato sauce
2 T.	flour
1-2	clove garlic

Freeze tofu, **thaw** and **press** out liquid. **Crumble. Add** to the above and heat through.

18	tortillas
2 c.	melty cheese
1 c.	diced peppers
1 c.	diced onion

Line 9 x 13 casserole with 6 tortillas, then ⅓ sauce, then ⅓ cheese, green pepper and onion. **Repeat** with tortillas, etc. **Sprinkle** with olive. **Bake** 45 minutes at 350°.

MEXICAN CORN CHOWDER

6	*servings*
1 c.	diced onion
½ c.	banana peppers
2 c.	fresh corn kernels (or canned corn)
1 c.	diced tomatoes (Mexican green tomatoes)
	salt to taste
3 c.	chicken-like
2 c.	soy or nut milk
½	red bell pepper (diced, for garnish)

Sauté onion in water with salt until translucent. Add peppers, green tomatoes, corn and chicken-like stock. **Cook** 10 to 15 minutes. **Puree** in blender. **Add** milk, bring to boil. **Taste**, adjust seasoning if necessary.

Garnish with diced red bell pepper in center of each bowl. 162 calories a serving.

SEASONED BEANS

10	*cups*
3 c.	soaked pinto beans (To soak, cover the beans with water overnight. Drain.)
9 c.	water
1 c.	green pepper
1 ½ c.	chopped onions
1 t.	salt
1 t.	cumin, optional
1 c.	tomato sauce

Combine all ingredients and **simmer** until beans are tender. Use beans for haystacks or any other Mexican dishes.

TACO CASSEROLE

12	*1 c. servings*
6 c.	cooked pinto beans
2 c.	kidney beans
1	large onion
2	large cloves of garlic
2 T.	salt
1 T.	cumin
½	pkg. Taco Seasoning (See Index)
2	recipes melty cheese

Mash beans in food processor. **Spread** them ½ or ⅓ in bottom of large baking dish. **Spoon** over this 1 c. Hunts Tomato Sauce Special or your favorite recipe. Then **add a** layer of melty cheese. Next a layer of corn tortillas. **Dribble** with melty cheese. Continue 1 or 2 times more. Bake at 350° for 40-45 minutes.

TACO CHIPS

48	*chips*
6	corn tortillas
	garlic powder
	onion powder

Preheat oven to 400°. **Cut** each tortilla into 8 triangles. **Place** triangles on a cake rack and **bake** six minutes. **Turn** the chips over. **Sprinkle** with garlic, onion, or both. **Bake** three minutes more.

TORTILLAS, flour

20	*tortillas*
2 c.	water
2 c.	rolled oats
¼ c.	sesame seeds
1 c.	whole wheat flour
2-3 c.	barley flour

Whiz water, rolled oats, and sesame seeds in blender until fine. **Pour** into a bowl and **add** the flour. **Knead**, then **roll** out small pieces into circles. **Bake** on a hot, ungreased griddle for one minute each side.

TOSTADAS SUPREME

6	*servings*
6	corn tortillas
2 c.	cooked or canned kidney or pinto beans, drained
1 t.	cumin powder
1 c.	tomato sauce
1	clove garlic, crushed or garlic powder

Garnishes:

2	green onions, chopped
1	large ripe tomato, chopped
1 c.	shredded lettuce or alfalfa sprouts
½ c.	(1 small can) sliced black olives
	Creamy Guacamole
	Salsa

Place tortillas on a baking sheet in a 300° oven and **bake** until crisp, about 10 minutes. **Season** beans with cumin, garlic and tomato sauce. **Cook** a few minutes, mashing beans. **Spread** tortillas with a layer of beans. **Top** beans with chopped green onions and tomato, then **add** melty cheese. **Bake** at 300° for about 5 minutes. **Serve**. Pass the garnishes.

Creamy Guacamole: **Mash** 2 ripe avocados in a mixing bowl. **Add** ½ c. tofu, a squeeze of lemon juice and 1 small clove garlic, crushed. For added zip, **season** with cumin or mild peppers to taste. **Mix** well.

Suggested meal additions: Raw vegetable platter or tossed salad, warm bread.

Norwegian

BEET SALAD IN ORANGE DRESSING

3-5	beets (about one bunch)

Dressing:

1 T.	date sugar
1	orange, juiced
3	scallions, sliced

Scrub the beets. **Simmer** for 30 minutes or until soft when pierced with fork. **Drain** beets, **rinse** under cool water. **Remove** the skins, and **slice** into thin rounds. **Mix** dressing in a small bowl, **pour** over beets, **stir**, and **adjust** flavors (you may need more juice). Allow flavors to marinate.

CABBAGE SALAD with Caraway

1	small cabbage, sliced thin
1/4	red cabbage, sliced thin

Dressing:

1/2 c.	grated onion
2 T.	lemon juice
2 T.	sesame seed-ground fine
1 T.	caraway seeds
pinch	sea salt
1/2 c.	chopped parsley or dill

Cut cabbage into wedges, then **slice** very thin. **Place** cabbage in a mixing bowl. **Grate** onion. **Add** all dressing ingredients to cabbage and **mix**. **Place** a plate on top of cabbage. Put a heavy jar on top of the plate to press the cabbage for a minimum of 1 hour. Cabbage becomes sweeter and softer the longer it is pressed. **Stir** before serving. **Save** juice for salad dressings.

GRATED CARROT SALAD

3-5	carrots, grated (about 4 cups)
1	lemon, juiced
2 T.	white grape juice
1 T.	olives, sliced or sesame seeds, ground
1/3 c.	chopped parsley
1/2 c.	sunflower seeds, roasted
	parsley sprigs for garnish

Grate the carrots. **Place** in a mixing bowl. **Add** the remaining ingredients and **stir** to coat evenly. **Adjust** salt and sour flavors by adding more lemon or sea salt. Allow to marinate for 1 hour. Keeps for 2 to 3 days.

NEW POTATO AND RED ONION SALAD

1	red onion, sliced thin
1 T.	lemon juice
5-7	new potatoes
2	stalks celery, sliced thin on a diagonal
pinch	salt

Dressing:

1/2 c.	mayonnaise
1/4 c.	chopped dill, basil or cilantro (optional)

Peel onion and **slice** very thin. **Place** onion in a mixing bowl and **sprinkle** with lemon. Allow red onions to "wilt" and become sweet. **Scrub** the potatoes. If they're large, **cut** in half or quarters. **Place** in a pot, **add** small amount of water and **bring** to a boil. **Simmer** on medium flame until soft, about 20 minutes. Don't overcook. **Drain** the potatoes. Allow to cool. **Peel** and **slice** thin while still warm and **add** to wilted red onions and celery. **Mix** the dressing in a small bowl. **Spoon** over salad. **Mix** gently to coat the vegetables. **Add** more dressing if needed. **Garnish** with slices of red radish and a sprig of watercress or parsley.

NORWEGIAN FLAT BREAD

1 c.	boiling water
2 1/2-3 c.	whole wheat flour
	(may use part unbleached flour and/or small amounts of other flours)
1/2 t.	salt
1 or 2	dates (optional)
	(may be blended in small amount of hot water to enhance the flavor)

Put flour and salt in a bowl. **Stir** well with a fork while **adding** the boiling water (with the dates, if desired) to make a stiff dough. **Mix** well and **knead** on the table to a soft, pliable dough, the consistency of yeast bread dough. **Add** a little more flour if it is too sticky. Using biscuit sized ball of dough, **roll** out very thin. **Bake** on cookie sheets in oven 350-375. (Hotter if one person can help watch to keep from burning, while the other person is rolling out the next one.) Do not get too brown. When "set", **remove** from cookie sheet and **place** on plain oven rack while it is still in oven, putting next one on cookie sheet. **Turn** over 1 or 2 times until lightly toasted. **Remove** from oven and **fold** in half immediately (while still soft) and let cool. Pieces can be opened to break in half for easier serving.

This is a small recipe—probably enough for 2 or 3 people.

SESAME SPREAD

⅓ c.	toasted sesame butter (or roasted tahini)
2 T.	soy sauce or equivalent
1	lemon, juiced
2-5	cloves garlic, minced (optional)
¼ t.	oregano powder or favorite herbs (optional)

Mix all ingredients in a small bowl or blender. **Add** more lemon juice or water if you prefer a creamier spread. **Store** in a jar and **refrigerate**. It will keep 3 to 5 days.

STRAWBERRY FLUFF

1 qt.	apple or strawberry-apple juice
½ c.	agar-agar flakes
pinch	sea salt
1 t.	vanilla
2	pints strawberries, rinsed and stems removed

Pour apple juice in a saucepan. **Sprinkle** the agar flakes over the juice and **add** a pinch of sea salt. Bring to a boil, and **simmer** on a low flame for 15 to 20 minutes, until the agar dissolves and **disappears**. **Stir** occasionally. **Add** vanilla. **Pour** juice into shallow glass dish or bowl. Allow to cool and set. It should become firm like gelatin.

Refrigerate or **chill**. When cold, **place** strawberries and cooked juice in a blender or food processor to whip to airy pinkness. Do this by placing a cup of berries and a cup of jelled juice together. **Puree** only to blend (not too much). **Serve** in dessert dishes. **Garnish** with whole or sliced strawberries. Keep refrigerated until ready to serve.

TOFU DILL SPREAD

8 oz.	tofu
2	scallions, minced
¼ c.	fresh dill, minced
1	dill pickle, minced (about 2 T.)
1-2 T.	pickle juice (as needed to blend)

Crumble tofu into a blender or food processor. **Blend** for 30 seconds. **Add** remaining ingredients. **Blend** to a creamy consistency. **Adjust** seasonings by adding more herbs or pickles.

TOFU TRIANGLES

6-8 oz.	tofu (one medium block)
2 T.	soy sauce or equivalent
1 t.	lemon juice

Slice tofu into ¼" pieces or triangles. **Drain** on paper towels to remove water. **Place** tofu in a small saucepan, **add** soy sauce or equivalent, lemon (plus any additional seasonings) and ¼ cup water. **Cover** and **simmer** for 3 to 5 minutes. Allow to cool before storing in containers.

DINNER MENU

Bread with filling—Bread dough rolled out in small squares; filled with cabbage, olive, onion, raisin mixture; and sealed. **Prick** top with fork to allow steam to escape when baking.

Salsa Blanca—Cauliflower blended and thickened if necessary for sauce for over the bread or beans.

Creamed corn—**Blend** in food processor. **Salt, garlic** to taste.

Cut green beans

Salad Bar:
1. Lettuce with carrots
2. Cucumber and onions minced with parsley and chopped green onions
3. Sliced tomatoes
4. Green onion dressing

PAELLA STYLE VEGETABLE

1 ½ c.	wild rice cooked in vegetable broth or chicken-like broth
1 c.	brown rice cooked as above
1	large onion, chopped
1	large green pepper, chopped
2-3	medium zucchini squash, sliced about ⅛" thick
1 lb.	broccoli, chopped and steam cooked not too soft
1 c.	green peas (frozen, cooked not too soft)
2	cloves garlic (or garlic powder)
½ t.	sweet red pepper
1 T.	oregano leaves
½ t.	anise
2	1 lb. cans tomatoes
1 T.	lemon juice

Cook onion and green pepper in tiny amount water until just tender (an electric skillet works well). **Add** zucchini squash and **cook** lightly. **Add** oregano, anise, garlic, sweet red pepper. **Mix** lightly and carefully. **Add** tomatoes, chopped in fourths. **Mix** lightly. (Add with juice.) **Add** cooked broccoli, peas, rice; **Mix** and **heat**. **Add** lemon.

Some recipes suggest that this can all be baked and cooked together but this gets the vegetables too soft. Spices may be altered to taste. May add blended cashews or cornstarch for thickening if you wish.

The Eight Natural Health Principles

Here at the Black Hills Health & Education Center, as we think of the eight natural health principles we think of **WELLNESS**.

W ater
E xercise
L ife-giving Air
L imits - Temperance
N utrition
E ssential Rest
S unlight
S piritual Dimension

Education in health principles is needed NOW. Our artificial way of living encourages the destruction of sound health principles. The practices and indulgences of today lessen both the physical and mental strength. Many transgress the laws of health unknowingly, but a great number know better than they do.

Poisonous drugs are the cause of much disease. Drugs do not cure disease. Sometimes they give present relief and the patient appears to recover as the result of their use. This is because nature has sufficient vital force to expel the poison and correct the conditions that cause the disease. Often the drug remains in the system and causes harm at a later time. Disease is an effort of nature to free the system from conditions that result from the violation of the laws of health. Everyone should understand healthful principles and know how to apply them.

The body is the only medium through which the mind is developed for the upbuilding of character. All need to be impressed with the fact that all powers of the mind and body are the gift of God and are to be preserved in the best possible condition for His service.

Now let us consider each remedy:

WATER – Pure water is one of heaven's choicest blessings. Its proper use promotes health. It is the beverage God provided to quench the thirst of animals and man. Drink it freely to help supply the necessities of the system and assist nature to resist disease. The external application of water is one of the easiest and most satisfactory ways of regulating the circulation of the blood. A cold or cool bath is an excellent tonic. Warm baths open the pores and thus aid in the elimination of impurities. Both warm and neutral baths soothe the nerves and equalize the circulation.

EXERCISE – Inactivity is a cause of disease. Exercise quickens and equalizes the circulation of the blood. In idleness the blood does not circulate freely. The skin becomes inactive. Impurities are not expelled, the skin is not kept in a healthy condition, nor the lungs fed with plenty of pure, fresh air, as they would be if the circulation had been quickened by vigorous exercise. This throws a double burden on the excretory organs, and disease results. Strictly temperate habits, combined with proper exercise, will ensure both mental and physical vigor. Invalids should not be encouraged in inactivity. Outdoor exercise is best. It should be planned so as to strengthen by use the organs that have become weakened. The labor of the hands should never degenerate into drudgery. Exercise gives the digestive organs a healthy tone. To engage in heavy study or strenuous exercise immediately after eating hinders the work of digestion, but a short walk after a meal, with the head erect and shoulders back is of great benefit.

LIFE-GIVING AIR – In order to have good blood we must breathe well. Full, deep inspirations of pure air, which fill the lungs with oxygen, purify the blood. A good respiration soothes the nerves, stimulates the appetite and makes digestion more perfect. It also induces sound, refreshing sleep. When the lungs do not receive sufficient oxygen, the blood moves sluggishly. The waste, poisonous matter, which should be thrown off in the exhalations from the lungs, is retained, and the blood becomes impure. Not only the lungs but the stomach, liver and brain are affected. Dwellings and public buildings should provide good ventilation and plenty of sunlight. Sleeping rooms should be so arranged as to have free circulation of air day and night. The lungs are constantly throwing off impurities and they need to be constantly supplied with fresh air.

LIMITS - TEMPERANCE – Strict temperance is a remedy for disease. Physical laws are not arbitrary—but if obeyed will be a blessing. Drink water, 6–8 glasses a day between meals. Exercise in the fresh air every day—walking is excellent. Breathe deeply of pure fresh air. Be temperate—not too little or too much of any one of the eight principles for wellness. We can overdo on even the good things in life! Eat enough good food, but not too much—only enough to maintain your proper weight. Be sure to rest sufficiently but at the proper time. Get out into the sunlight but do not get a sunburn. All of these principles were given to us by God so that the body may be kept in health.

NUTRITION – Intemperance in eating is often the cause of sickness; and what the body needs most is to be relieved of the undue burden that has been placed upon it. In many cases of sickness, the very best remedy is for the patient to fast for a meal or two that the overworked organs of digestion may have an opportunity to rest. A fruit diet for a few days has often brought relief to brain workers. Many times a short period of entire abstinence from food, followed by simple, moderate eating has led to recovery through nature's own recuperative effort. An abstemious diet for a month or two would convince many that the path of self-denial is the path to health.

Fresh fruits and vegetables, raw, should be included in our daily menu as well as the cooked. Whole grains in main dishes, breads, crackers, etc., should also be included. Nuts and avocados should be used in smaller amounts—one-sixth to one-tenth part of nuts in casseroles or other products.

ESSENTIAL REST – Some make themselves sick by overwork. For these, rest, freedom from care, and a spare diet are essential to restoration of health. To those who are brain-weary and nervous because of continual labor and close confinement, a visit to the country, where they can live a simple, carefree life, coming in close contact with the things of nature, will be most helpful. Roaming through the fields and woods, picking flowers, listening to the song of the birds, will do far more than any other agency toward their recovery.

SUNLIGHT – Sunlight is one of the most healing agents given to all on this earth. It has a tremendous impact on the mental and emotional well-being. It would be well to plan to walk or work out in the sunlight whenever possible for maximum benefits. Let the sun shine into the home. Accept it as a gift from God and worship the Creator.

SPIRITUAL DIMENSION – Within each person there is a desire to worship Someone. The understanding, the will, the affections, must be yielded to the control of the Word of God. Then through the Holy Spirit the precepts of the Word will become the principles of the life. Walk continually in the light of God. Meditate day and night upon His character. Then you will see His beauty and rejoice in His goodness. With the power and light that God imparts, you can comprehend more and accomplish more than you ever before thought possible.

Happy are we if we know these things and do them. *(John 13:17)*

(Much of the material on **WELLNESS** will be found in "Ministry of Healing" by E. G. White.)

Index

Natural Sweets

Miscellaneous

Seasonings

From Other Countries

Chinese

East Indian

Greek

Italian

Mexican

Norwegian

South American-Peru

Alphabetical Index

Face the future...

at the BLACK HILLS MISSIONARY COLLEGE

Four Year Degree Programs:
- Elementary Education
- Secondary Education
- Health Promotion and Physical Fitness
- Nutrition/Food Service Management
- Religion and Biblical Languages
- Pastoral Ministries, Health/Religion
- Interdisciplinary Christian Studies

Two Year Degree Programs:
- Food Service
- Health Science
- Personal Ministries
- Agriculture

Develop your skills for professional Christian service in one of the Associate or Bachelor's degree programs available at BLACK HILLS MISSIONARY COLLEGE.

Write to: Dean
Black Hills Missionary College
Box 3700
Rapid City, SD 57701

or call: 605-255-4104
1-800-658-5433

Located in Vacation Land!

AVAILABLE for your convenience and cooking pleasure:

COOKING WITH NATURAL FOODS - cookbook

COOKING WITH NATURAL FOODS II - cookbook

COOKING WITH NATURAL FOODS RECIPE CARD COLLECTION in an attractive ACRYLIC BOX with a protective shield for the recipe when in use.

COOKING WITH NATURAL FOODS II, RECIPE CARD COLLECTION that will fit in the box with the other recipes.

ORDER BLANKS:

- -

I would like _____ copy or copies of *COOKING WITH NATURAL FOODS* at $14.95, postpaid.

I would like _____ copy or copies of *COOKING WITH NATURAL FOODS II* at $14.95, postpaid.

I would like _____ set or sets of *COOKING WITH NATURAL FOODS RECIPE CARD COLLECTION* **in the attractive acrylic box** at $29.95 (plus postage of $5.00). Cards only—$24.95, postpaid.

I would like _____ set or sets of *COOKING WITH NATURAL FOODS II RECIPE CARD COLLECTION* at $24.95, postpaid. (These will fit in the box with the first set of recipes.)

Please send them as soon as possible. My check ☐ or money order ☐ in the amount of _____ is enclosed.

Date _____ Signed _____

Mailing Address _____

Please remit U.S. currency.

Make check to **B.H.H.E.C.** and send with the order to:

Muriel Beltz, Black Hills Health and Education Center, HCR 89, Box 167, Hermosa, South Dakota 57744 Telephone: 605-255-4789, 255-4101 or 255-9717

- -

I would like _____ copy or copies of *COOKING WITH NATURAL FOODS* at $14.95, postpaid.

I would like _____ copy or copies of *COOKING WITH NATURAL FOODS II* at $14.95, postpaid.

I would like _____ set or sets of *COOKING WITH NATURAL FOODS RECIPE CARD COLLECTION* **in the attractive acrylic box** at $29.95 (plus postage of $5.00). Cards only—$24.95, postpaid.

I would like _____ set or sets of *COOKING WITH NATURAL FOODS II RECIPE CARD COLLECTION* at $24.95, postpaid. (These will fit in the box with the first set of recipes.)

Please send them as soon as possible. My check ☐ or money order ☐ in the amount of _____ is enclosed.

Date _____ Signed _____

Mailing Address _____

Please remit U.S. currency.

Make check to **B.H.H.E.C.** and send with the order to:

Muriel Beltz, Black Hills Health and Education Center, HCR 89, Box 167, Hermosa, South Dakota 57744 Telephone: 605-255-4789, 255-4101 or 255-9717

LOVE NOTES: What others have said—

"I am excited about the prospect of some day coming to the Black Hills Center . . . Thank you for your work and for taking time to respond to my letters. Also thank you for letting the Lord use you to answer prayers in New Jersey. Without your help, recipes and encouragement, I'd still be wallowing in fats and sugars!" New Jersey

"Would you please send me a list and prices on your cookbook or whatever else you might have. I really would appreciate it." Wisconsin

"I hope you will be able to use these recipes. I'll be anxious to see your new cookbook." Iowa

"If you are ever in our area with your seminars, please come to visit us. Our home is open to you and we cook some pretty good and healthful meals. How can I go wrong when I've got the BEST cookbook—**Cooking With Natural Foods**." New Jersey

"I personally wish to thank you and others for the plan developed, Cooking With Natural Foods recipes, etc. My husband has lost 21 pounds and I have lost 14 pounds, and we eat like kings and queens and love it! May God be praised!" Wisconsin

"Thank you for sending your lovely cookbook. I know I am going to enjoy using it. Cooking healthfully is an exciting challenge." Wisconsin